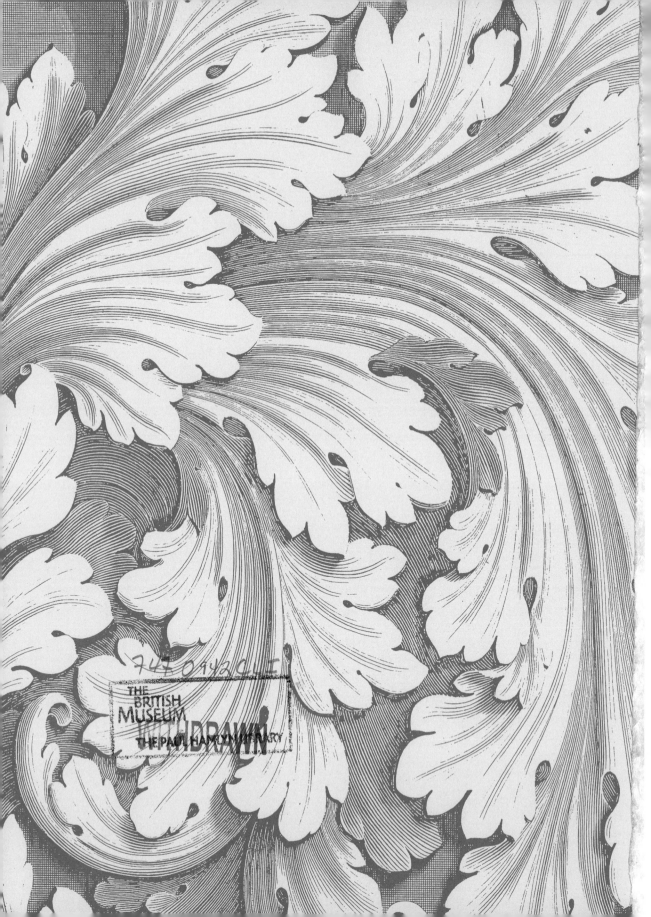

ENGLISH
STYLE AND
DECORATION

530.

531.

532.

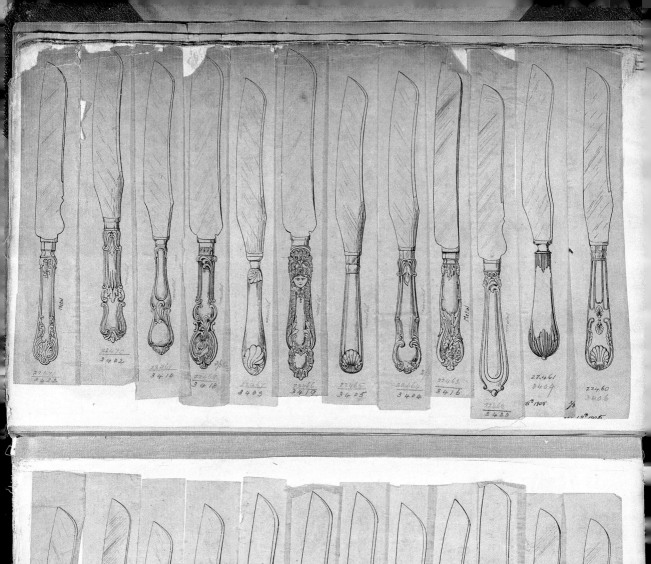

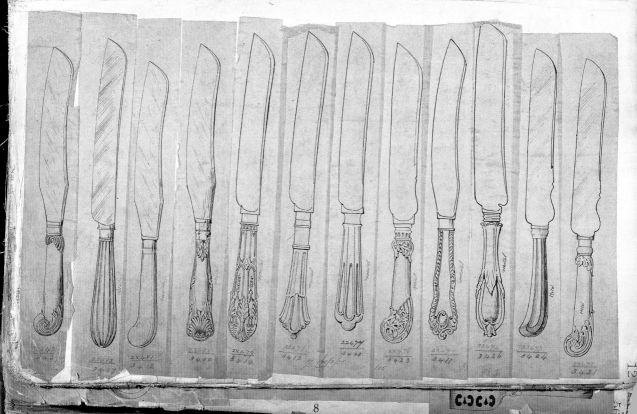

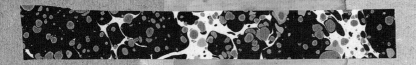

Author's
PREFACE

Half-title, Title and Contents Pages and Pages 6–7

The archive of the Spode pottery and porcelain factory in Stoke-on-Trent is a repository of English design genius from the 18th century to the present. Though one pattern record book from the time of the foundation of the company in 1776 by Josiah Spode I still exists, most of the well-worn volumes date from 1800, when the decorating department was established. Each page bears a hand-painted record of a pattern with its appropriate number. In spite of several changes in the ownership of the company, this extraordinary heirloom of design has remained intact.

These pages (pp. 6-7) from a master pattern book of 1804 record a sugar basin and cover, a coffee can and a 'Bute' shape teacup, decorated on-glaze in gold. Every pattern, when produced, was given a pattern number (there are 70,000 on record) which were sometimes stamped on the wares. The design of this coffee cup 531 was revived in 1950 in gold on dark blue and incorporated into the Arundel range.

opposite Early twentieth-century designs for bread knives from Elkington & Co., Birmingham.

This book is a celebration of the work of the named and unnamed artist-designers who made such an astonishing and original contribution to English domestic culture, craftsmanship and manufacture during the eighteenth, nineteenth and early twentieth centuries. Although it is formally divided into periods reflecting changes in the design and style concerns of the nation, it is neither a formal history nor a comprehensive directory of them. The brief introductions to each section are intended simply to provide the background against which the illustrations that follow can be seen and appreciated. Within each section I have grouped the designs visually, sometimes relating similar work by different artists, sometimes contrasting different solutions to similar problems, sometimes showing consecutive pages from the same documents, and elsewhere putting unrelated schemes side by side because of their visual rapport.

During my researches, some of the records I discovered could hardly have been expected to survive, being little more than scraps of paper, never intended for a client's eyes, let alone to be printed in a book. Other designs I found recorded in pattern books, swatch books, shape books, sometimes actually rendered in colour by the very craftsmen who had earlier made the finished artefact. Such records often showed the signs of constant use: the worn edges of pages marked with potters' clay or even singed by a glass-blower's flame; patterns annotated with later comments or artisans' instructions; bindings battered by constant handling. Yet, for the most part, the designs still reveal the remarkable skills of those who drew them, and a freshness and spontaneity as appealing today as when they were first created.

NTRODUCTION

Between 1700 and 1939 England and English
design held a pre-eminent position in the applied arts of the
western world, creating a unique national heritage. Simply
to mention some of the major names of this long and
complex period – Kent, Chippendale, Hepplewhite, Adam,
Sheraton, Pugin, Morris, Voysey, Liberty, Gimson – is to
evoke a history and an achievement rarely equalled at any
time in the decorative arts. The furniture and interiors of
these designers have had world-wide influence; even when
industrialization transformed and expanded the making of
household materials and artefacts in the nineteenth century,
the pattern books and catalogues of English firms remained
the source of a multiplicity of elegant solutions to practical problems.

The names of Chippendale and Liberty could perhaps be taken as twin peaks of
English achievement in design, one in the initial period and the other in the latter of the
timespan covered by this book, both establishing their reputation by the dissemination
of published matter about their creations. In 1754, Thomas Chippendale issued his *The
Gentleman and Cabinet-maker's Director*. As well as being a record of contemporary
style and taste, it was an advertisement for Chippendale's own work and a source-book
for jobbing craftsmen throughout the world. At the end of the nineteenth century and
the beginning of the twentieth the catalogues for furniture, textiles, pottery and glass
of the London shop of Liberty established such a high reputation for the firm's products
and retailing practices that the term 'Liberty' came to designate *fin-de-siècle* design in
both France and Italy.

Yet, a nation's design heritage is made up of much more than a few well-known
names. Behind the pattern books of nineteenth-century manufacturers lies the work
of scores of anonymous draughtsmen and craftsmen responsible for thousands of
original designs, whose uncredited work often displays great artistic flair and technical

ingenuity. Some of the names of designers whose work is included in the illustration pages of this book will be immediately recognizable as the taste-formers of their age. But many of the most interesting, imaginative and beautiful works are by those whose individuality remained unrecognized by the workshops and manufacturers which employed them.

The illustrations in this book have, therefore, been drawn from a variety of sources: design books, pattern books, shape books, swatch books, company archives, manufacturers' and retail catalogues. Many companies maintained comprehensive archives and design records until World War II, after which time some were lodged for safe keeping in public collections. These often consisted of books of original designs and sketches recording the used and unused motifs and forms over a given period and were therefore intended essentially for internal use. Such records provided a source and inspiration for further design and production years after their creation, especially in the case of those firms, notably in wallpaper, textile and pottery manufacture, whose reputation depended on the continuity of a certain English 'look'. A textile mill, for instance, would maintain a record of its production in the form of swatch books. These may contain the artist's original designs and sometimes trial impressions of printing on paper before application to a particular fabric. It is common, too, to find such books with actual cuttings from the cloth – swatches – as originally printed.

Clearly, such records were never intended for public use, and the beauty and extent of much of this material has only come to be appreciated since its appearance either on the open market at auction, in public archives, in exhibition and in publications such as *The World of Interiors*.

Much more directly accessible were manufacturers' catalogues, which contain records of a company's output and are therefore representations of post-production artefacts rather than pre-production design; these were intended for the use of sales representatives and the eventual customer or retailer. Late eighteenth-century sample books were rarely dated and bore no maker's name or title-page information. They were carried from town to town by itinerant agents who carefully guarded their own sources of manufacture and a network of contacts often built up over years. The cost and scarcity

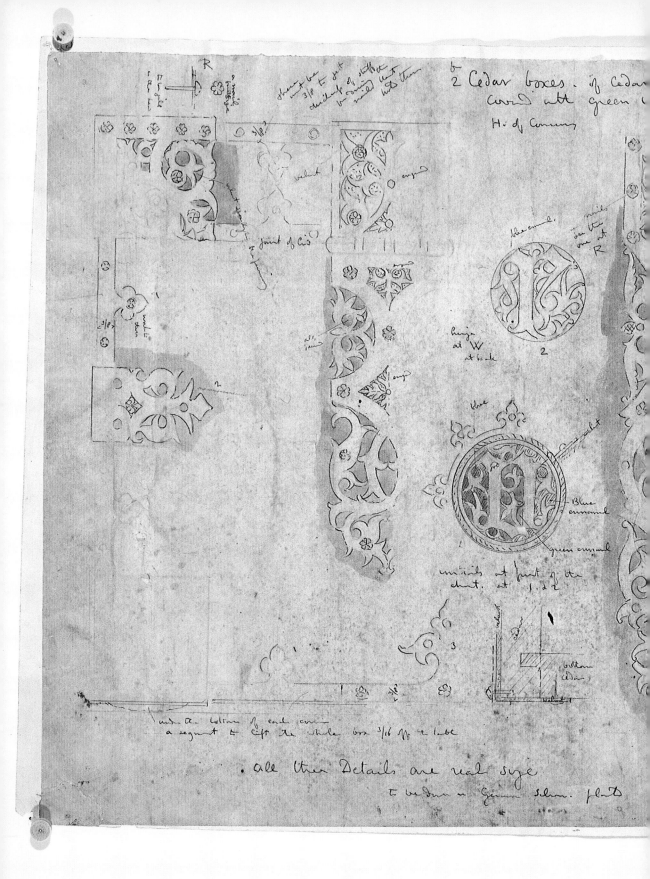

2 Cedar boxes. of Cedar
Cover'd with green

H. of Corners

all their Details are real size
to be done in German silver plate

of raw materials and poor state of the road network undoubtedly contributed to the growth of such secretive practices, but the anonymity of the books meant that clients found it hard to approach manufacturers directly and the lack of a date disguised to provincial eyes the fact that a style was out-dated.

In the early nineteenth century the customer may very well have been an architect-designer or 'upholsterer' (the equivalent of today's interior designer) who would employ craftsmen as well as purchasing furnishings and fittings, often for the new town and country houses of the burgeoning upper middle and middle classes. As industrialization grew in the production of domestic equipment and artefacts, so too did the production of catalogues aimed at suppliers to a mass market. These would often take the form of fragments of the finished object (wallpapers or textiles, for instance), rather than drawings or paintings.

A later development of such promotion of wares to both a specialized and general public was the issuing of store and shop catalogues. In the late nineteenth century and the early decades of the twentieth both Liberty and Heal's produced exciting anthologies of furniture, textiles and other objects, often specially created for the firm, which promoted a particular design ethos and helped to imprint a distinctly English look on the international design consciousness.

Another important category of pattern book, and one substantially represented here, is that of the publication intended both as a register of current fashion and also as an inspiration to the craftsman and the would-be decorator. In the early eighteenth century such books, containing engraved designs for ceilings, doorways and chimneypieces, were issued by architects and builders. The practice soon spread to the publication of designs for furniture, although it should be noted that some of the earliest examples of this were inspired by foreign craftsmen working in London, notably by the Italian Brunetti and the Frenchman De La Cour. Outstanding English pattern books of the period include Matthew Lock's *Six Sconces* of 1744 and his *Six Tables* of 1746, followed in 1752 by his *New Book of Ornaments*. Undoubtedly the finest eighteenth-century example of such publishing, however, is Thomas Chippendale's *Director*, which began a tradition to be followed by other famous English designers, decorators and furniture-makers: Thomas Johnson, George Hepplewhite and Thomas Sheraton.

In the nineteenth century, books, catalogues and journals devoted to the publication of styles, patterns and whole decorative schemes proliferated, which partly explains the wild eclecticism of much of early and mid Victorian domestic design. Robert Bridgens' *Furniture and Candelabra and Interior Decoration* of 1838, for instance, lists twenty-seven 'Elizabethan' designs, twenty-five 'Grecian', and seven 'Gothic'. Later examples of this type of publication do, however, show the influence of the great Victorian design reformers in the movement towards a more homogeneous approach to interior design and a greater respect for material and suitability of form. William Godwin, notably, created designs for an *Art Furniture* catalogue in 1877; in 1880, T. Knight and Sons published *Suggestions for Home Decoration*, which included whole room settings in a variety of styles. Later, the Arts and Crafts Movement was to take the concept of total domestic design much further, wherein every detail became a carefully considered part of a whole domestic environment. For these later periods, many of the original designs have survived and were, in any case, copiously reproduced, notably in the pages of *The Studio*.

The accumulation of design archives and the variety of publishing which accompanied the activities of designers, craftsmen and manufacturers throughout the eighteenth and nineteenth centuries were clearly not phenomena confined solely to the market in domestic artefacts. Such processes also aided the expansion of industrial, commercial and ecclesiastical design and knowledge. Yet, to have included so many different types of design in the present book would certainly have diluted our central concern: to demonstrate by comparative illustration the strength of the English domestic design tradition and the skills to record such design through nearly two and a half centuries. From whatever source they are taken – original sketchbook, pattern book, manufacturer's or retailer's catalogue, and even scraps of paper – the illustrations here have been chosen because they show exciting, occasionally very ingenious, solutions to design problems as perceived at a given time. They are all interesting, and frequently very beautiful. They have an immediacy, even to the contemporary eye, and are therefore equally relevant to the search for design inspiration today.

400 cords No 8 & 11 — Ap: 28th 1721 — for Mr Alexander
Deaines Simples —

CLASSICISM
and ROCOCO

The development of the English applied arts in the
eighteenth century is very much a history of alternating
taste: classical simplicity, succeeded by the decorative
exuberance of a native form of Rococo, and then back
to a regard for stricter forms in Neoclassicism.

One name above all informed English attitudes to
design in the early part of the century: that of Andrea
Palladio, the Italian Renaissance architect. Two
publications of 1715 helped underline his pre-eminent
position as an exemplar of fine taste in the applied arts:
Colin Campbell's *Vitruvius Britannicus*, which delineated
the development of the large country house in England
in a series of engravings, and an English translation of
the Italian master's own *Four Books of Architecture*.
This work had been a considerable source of inspiration
to the earlier English architect, Inigo Jones, whose work
had come to be much admired by both patrons and
architects in the early eighteenth century.

Political and social factors also contributed to the
vogue for a muted classicism in the early eighteenth
century. Firstly, there was a Hanoverian, George I, on
the throne and the Whig party supreme in Parliament –
a combination which tended, expectedly, to promote a
certain sobriety of taste. Secondly, the very architects
who so admired the balanced proportions of Palladio
began at this time to assume a much more
prominent role in all fields of domestic design,
taking over from guild-organized craftsmen; the latter,
by and large, had not committed their designs to paper

in any publishable form. In contrast, the new generation of architect-designers went out of their way to make sure that their plans, decorative schemes, details of ornaments and furniture were disseminated to a wider public in books of engravings published by themselves, usually with the sponsorship of a noble patron.

A new emphasis on formal entertaining began to emerge in the early part of the eighteenth century; this intensified the demand for integrated decorative schemes in the main rooms of great houses. Country house and town house visiting became a distinct social practice during the century; there are records, for instance, of Josiah Wedgwood visiting the London houses of the aristocracy and gentry as potential sources of new design ideas.

Typical of the new type of patron was the young Lord Burlington who spent much of the second decade of the century in Italy, studying the work of Palladio. He was also the patron of William Kent, the pre-eminent English architect-designer of the early eighteenth century, whose publication of *The Designs of Inigo Jones* in 1727 did much to reinforce the prevailing classical taste in all aspects of design. Ironically, Kent's own interior decoration and furniture design have a flamboyance and opulence which make more than a gesture towards the Baroque of the previous century.

The growing importance of pattern-books in the forming of taste through the dissemination of 'fashionable' designs has already been remarked on in the general introduction to this book. And it is through pattern-books that the development of mid-century taste for the lighter forms of Rococo can most readily be seen. Even as early as 1739, *The Gentlemen's or Builder's Companion*, published by the architect William Jones, contained some examples of carved furniture more suggestive of Louis Quinze than English Palladianism. But it was the publication of Chippendale's *The Gentleman and Cabinet-maker's Director* in 1754 which almost certainly ensured the widest possible dissemination of the new trends in taste. Almost all the 160 engraved plates are devoted to furniture designs, some incorporating Gothic and Oriental motifs (which also enjoyed renewed vogues in the middle of the century), but the main decorative repertoire is drawn from the sinuous curves, carved scrolls and flowers of Rococo.

More Rococo designs appeared in 1755 in *Twelve Gerandoles* by Thomas Johnson, which contained designs for wall lights in gilded wood – a form of ornament which lent itself particularly well to the swirling lines of the prevailing fashion. Johnson later published a second edition, entitled *One Hundred and Fifty New Designs*, which contained a wealth of exotic motifs in settings of scrolls and leafy branches. Another important publication of the time was Ince and Mayhew's *The Universal System*

of *Household Furniture* of 1762 which included a wide range of designs for cabinet-makers in the Rococo style.

Of all the designers who published their pattern books, it was Chippendale who seems to have had the most sensitive feel for changing tastes. When the third edition of his *Director* appeared in 1762 with 105 new plates, it was apparent that he had divined that a return to the classicism of the early part of the century was imminent and that the days of Rococo, however immediately charming, were numbered. In this ability to recognize shifts of taste, he must be accounted one of the central figures in the history of design and style of the eighteenth century.

The new Neoclassicism was taken up and disseminated widely by the Adam brothers, both in their work as domestic architects and decorators and in their folio volume of engravings published in 1777, *The Works in Architecture of Robert and James Adam*. Thousands of drawings by Robert are now preserved in the Soane Museum in London, providing a unique record of English style in the latter half of the eighteenth century. One notable contribution of Robert Adam to the development of design was his concern to provide artefacts which complemented his furniture and interiors. In his designs for Osterley Park, for instance, he provided for a complete range of meticulously detailed dining equipment.

The demand for the new style had extended well beyond London and the great houses by the penultimate decade of the century. Craftsmen and small firms of cabinet-makers in the provinces were well-served, however, in 1788 with the publication of *The Cabinet-maker and Upholsterer's Guide*, which made the elegant forms and motifs of English Neoclassicism available to a wide audience. Originally assembled by George Hepplewhite, who died in 1786, it was published posthumously by his widow. Although it was principally devoted to furniture design, it is easy to see that it could have served as a source-book for a wide range of domestic design in its display of Neoclassical ornament: husks, festoons, swags and grotesques.

The success of the Hepplewhite book probably inspired the publication of the last great design book of the century, *The Cabinet-maker and Upholsterer's Drawing Book* by Thomas Sheraton, published in four parts between 1791 and 1794. The cool elegance of the designs, the gentle emphases of flower and leaf patterns, the gracefully tapering legs provide a modulated but eminently satisfying finale to a century of fine English design.

page 16 A silk design by James Leman (*c.* 1688-1745) dated 1721; it is accompanied by the names of the mercer and the journeyman-weaver.

opposite Glass-blowers at work: an etching published in 1754 in *The Dictionary of Arts and Sciences.*

1

CLASSICISM
and
ROCOCO

pages 20–21

An interesting example of mid-century English Rococo, this design for a drawing room by John Linnell (1723-96) reflects the designer's knowledge of furniture-making; his father, William Linnell, had established a successful upholstery and cabinet-making business in Berkeley Square, London. Later furniture designs by Linnell were influenced by the prevailing taste for Chinoiserie (see p. 31).

page 25

The pre-eminent architect-designer of early eighteenth-century England was undoubtedly William Kent (1684-1748). His architectural work and drawings, like this front elevation and ground plan, did much to reinforce the classical taste of the time, although his interior design had an opulence which looked more, perhaps, towards the Baroque of the previous century.

pages 26–27

The alternation of preferences for the frivolity of Rococo or for the more sober lines of Palladian classicism continued throughout the middle part of the eighteenth century. French artists, too, came to work in England when the more decorative style became less fashionable in France; these included Andien de Clermont who executed this ceiling design for Langley Park, Norfolk, *c.* 1750.

pages 28–29

The design of chair backs provides a wonderful barometer of taste through the century. This sketch by John Linnell (p. 28) has a wonderful mid-century exuberance and freshness and was probably executed as a preliminary design for pieces to be made by his father's company. The designs by Thomas Chippendale (1718-79) (p. 29 *above*) are the preliminary pencil sketches for the third edition of his *The Gentleman and Cabinet-maker's Director* (1762), which mixed the curves and scrolls of the first edition (1754) with designs which reflected a renewed classicism. This spirit continued in furniture to the refined Neoclassicism of the latter part of the century, notably in the graceful elegance of designs (p. 29 *below*) by Thomas Sheraton (1751-1806), whose *The Cabinet-maker and Upholsterer's Drawing Book* was published between 1791 and 1794.

pages 30/32–33

Born in Sweden of Scottish parents, but educated in England, William Chambers (1723-96) travelled extensively in the Far East. His close acquaintanceship with Chinese architecture and design inspired his first published work, *Designs of Chinese Buildings, Furniture, Dresses, Machines, and Utensils* (1757), from which these pages are taken. The publication of the book was timely indeed, since it coincided with a period of intense interest among wealthy patrons in the Chinoiserie aspects of Rococo. At about the same time Chambers designed the Pagoda in Kew Gardens (see p. 51).

page 31

The taste for Chinoiserie reached its peak just as the mid-century fashion for the Rococo style was at its most intense, profoundly influencing design in furniture, textiles and porcelain. This little watercolour painting of an armchair in the Chinese style by John Linnell, again probably for use in his father's workshops, dates from *c.* 1753.

pages 34–35

The spare classicism which characterized English design in the early part of the eighteenth century is marvellously expressed in two chimney-piece designs in pen, ink and wash by Christopher Cass (1678-1734). The first (p. 34) was intended for Vanbrugh's Blenheim Palace, the second for Hampton Court (p. 35).

pages 36–37

The eighteenth-century demand for complete decorative schemes in the main public rooms and spaces of great houses provided the impetus for many architects and artists to become, effectively, interior designers. Many of the original sketches have an engaging vigour and confidence, such as the design for the interior of a drawing room (p. 36 *above*), by Thomas Stothard (1755-1834), which demonstrates scale by the inclusion of sketched human figures. James Stuart's design for Wimbledon House (p. 36 *below*) makes greater use

1

CLASSICISM
and
ROCOCO

of classical motifs. Known as 'Athenian' Stuart, this architect (1713-88) exerted a strong influence on the maintenance of the classical ideal in England through his co-authorship of *The Antiquities of Athens* (1762-89) and his interiors in a Roman style for Spencer House, London. Some sense of the relationship between such architect- designers and their clients can be gained from Sir James Thornhill's (1676-1734) design for a staircase, probably for the house of his mentor, Thomas Highmore (p. 37); in the upper right-hand corner of the sketch, the painter has listed the proposed combinations of figures and events from mythology and classical history for approval. Thornhill was responsible for several grand illusionist painting schemes, notably at Chatsworth.

pages 38–39

The name of Gillow recurs repeatedly in the history of English furniture design and manufacture from the eighteenth century to the twentieth. Originally established *c.* 1730 in Lancaster by Robert Gillow (1703-73), the firm added a London branch *c.* 1765 on a site in Oxford Street occupied by their successors,

Waring & Gillow, until 1974. In their eighteenth-century heyday Gillow produced elegant, well-made furniture in the late Georgian style, typified by the sofa and writing-table designs illustrated on these pages. The company maintained, and jealously guarded, a comprehensive record of its production from 1734 to 1899, comprising some 20,000 designs; the extent and variety of this unique compilation contained in successive sketches only came to be properly appreciated in 1966, when it was acquired by the Westminster City Library.

pages 40–41

Matthew Darly (*fl.* 1741-80) was one of the most notable English furniture designers to be influenced by the fashionable French Rococo style. He was also influential in spreading the taste for Chinoiserie, especially by his 1751 pattern book, *A New Book of Chinese, Gothic and Modern Chairs*, from which these eight designs are taken. Darly was also an engraver and made most of the plates for Chippendale's 1754 *Director*. In that year, too, he published *A New Book of Chinese Designs*.

pages 42–43

This spare, classical design for a tallboy (p. 43) forms Plate 86 in the 1754 edition of Thomas Chippendale's *Director*, undoubtedly the seminal pattern book of the 18th century and the means of ensuring that Chippendale's name became a household word as England's most eminent furniture designer. The *Director* illustrated virtually every type of domestic furniture in a variety of styles, though mainly (unlike the piece illustrated here) Rococo and Chinoiserie, known as Chinese Chippendale. His sensitivity to changing taste was amply illustrated in the third edition of the *Director* which showed a shift to more Neoclassical sympathies. Another of the great eighteenth-century pattern books was George Hepplewhite's *The Cabinet-maker and Upholsterer's Guide*, published by the designer's widow in 1788, two years after her husband's death. The furniture epitomizes the Neoclassicism of the latter part of the 18th century. The designs, such as this one for a wardrobe (p. 42), have an elegant simplicity and must have been one of the principal sources of inspiration for

cabinet-makers throughout the country for the whole of the latter part of the century.

pages 44–45

The growth in importance of the architect-designer in eighteenth-century England could not be better illustrated than on these pages. A wealthy and well-travelled aristocracy and a powerful merchant class demanded new building, both in town and country, and with the building came the demand for complete integrated design, outside and inside. These anonymous sketches (p. 44) of Elton hall, Northamptonshire, show an extraordinary overlapping of plans and elevations for a complex of buildings, including an orangery, all drawn on a small scrap of sketchbook paper. The more finished treatments by Robert Adam (1728-92) for town-house elevations, front and back, in central London (p. 45) bespeak the Neoclassical influences which the architect absorbed during a four-year period spent in Rome. Adam was in many ways the complete designer, continuing the elegance of his architecture through to free-standing furniture, wall and ceiling decoration (see pp. 52-53).

1
CLASSICISM
and
ROCOCO

pages 46–47

The exchange and intermingling of highly ornate decorative styles and design of classical simplicity constitutes much of the history of eighteenth-century English design. This counterpointing is succinctly illustrated by the contrasting designs on these pages. Samuel Savill's sketched records (p. 47) have the sobriety of the classical models he clearly admired. Matthew Lock's original designs for free-standing and wall furniture (p. 46), on the other hand, have the exuberance and frivolity expected of a designer who played a leading part in introducing the Rococo style to England. His *A New Drawing Book of Ornaments* of 1740 was one of the first pattern books to promote this style in London. It was followed by *Six Sconces* (1744) and *Six Tables* (1746).

pages 48–49

Neoclassical elegance informs even these prosaically utilitarian artefacts of *c.* 1790. The Miles Patent Agitable Lamp came in several forms to suit both taste and position. Oil-burning, it was claimed to be free from spillage even when carried about. It was advertised as being 'cleaner, safer, and cheaper than candles' in the manufacturer's catalogue, which also showed one model which could be strapped to a horse-rider's calf.

pages 50–51

William Pain, the designer of the mouldings illustrated on p. 50, originally a carpenter by trade, commented on the vigorous state of English architecture in his *Practical Builder* (1774), presumably only too conscious that this was partly due to the influence exercised by such books as his. Indeed, the pattern books of English architects and builders began to have a transatlantic influence in the late 18th century. An American edition of Pain's own *Practical House Carpenter* was published in 1792, to become one of the most influential works for the classical architects of New England. A much more eminent contemporary of Pain's was William Chambers (see pp. 30/32-33) who became one of the most successful architects in England, designing – notably – Somerset House in London. Two years after his first book, *Designs of Chinese Buildings*, he produced his most influential published work, the *Treatise on Civil Architecture*, from which this illustration of mouldings is taken (p. 51). The book concentrated entirely on the decorative and design aspects of building and interior design, eventually reaching an expanded third edition in 1791 as *A Treatise on the Decorative Part of Civil Architecture*.

pages 52–53

These two sketches by Robert Adam (p. 52) for the wall decoration of 17 Hill Street, London, have a lightness, freshness and frivolity almost more in keeping with the spirit of the mid-century than with that of the later Neoclassicism. Festoons and scrolls distinguish him from the severity of his French contemporaries, as does the lightness of the palette he used for plasterwork. Note the precise instructions for colour contrast. A similar lightness of touch characterizes Adam's sketch for a balustrade 'for Lady Home' of 1777 (p. 53).

pages 54–55

Although the 18th century in English design ended on a distinctly classical note, it had overall been a time of eclecticism and marvellous design ingenuity and fantasy. The 1762 edition of Chippendale's *Director* still carried designs very much in the Rococo style (p. 54), while Thomas Johnson (1714-*c.* 1778) specifically devoted himself to designing the decorative elements known as 'carvers' pieces', which excluded larger pieces and chairs, concentrating on chimneypieces (p. 55), mirror frames, side tables and other decorative artefacts. His designs, strongly inspired by French models, were probably too intricate to have been fully realized by any carver, but his books went a long way to establishing the decorative style as a major theme in eighteenth-century English design. *Twelve Gerandoles* was published in 1755, with a further set following in parts during the next two years. These designs were eventually issued in volume form in 1758 and, slightly expanded, in 1761 as *One Hundred and Fifty New Designs*.

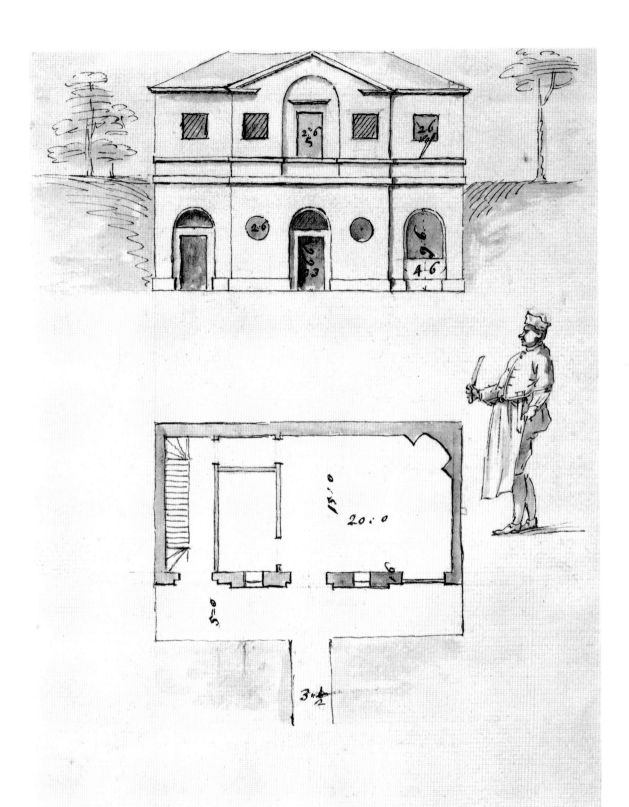

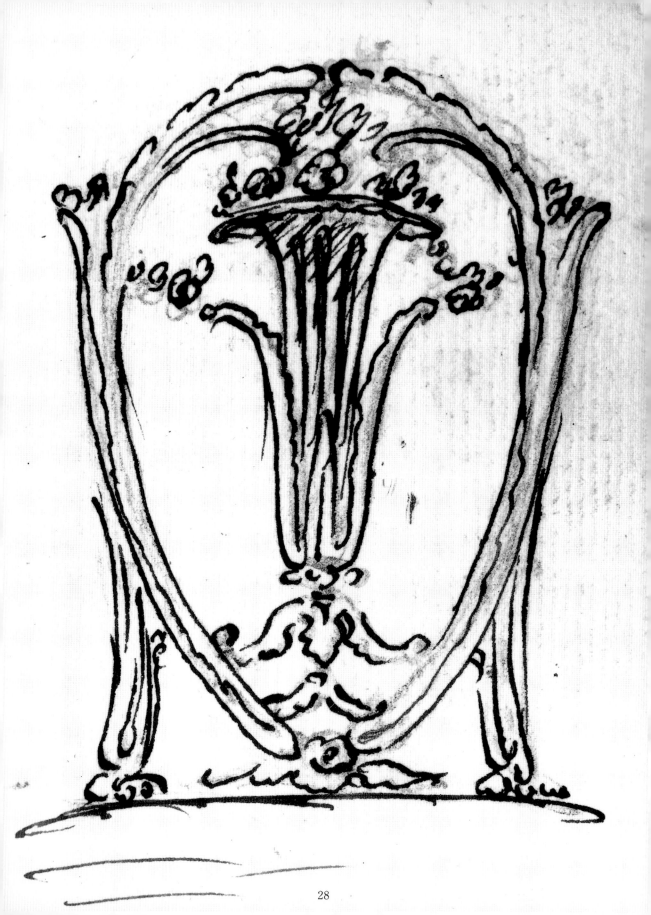

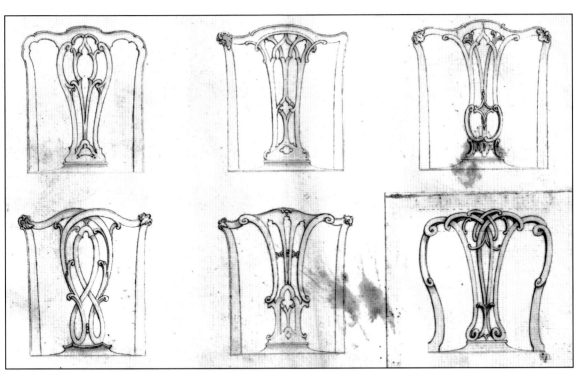

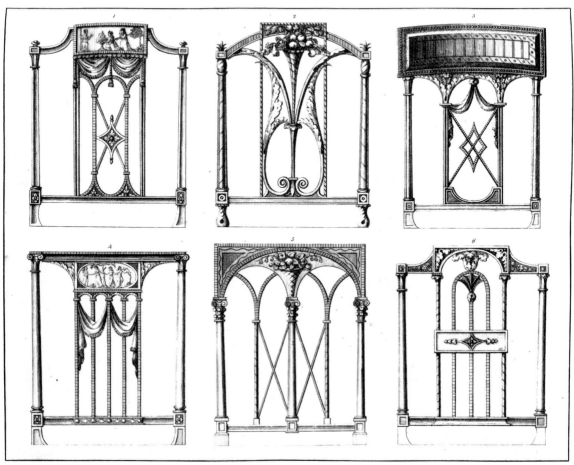

E 71 11/9

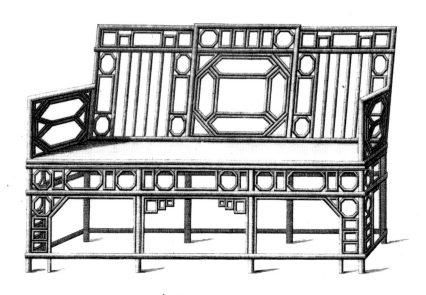
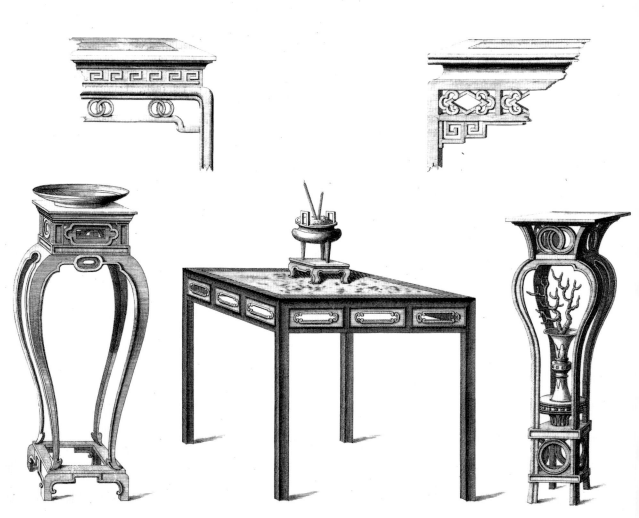

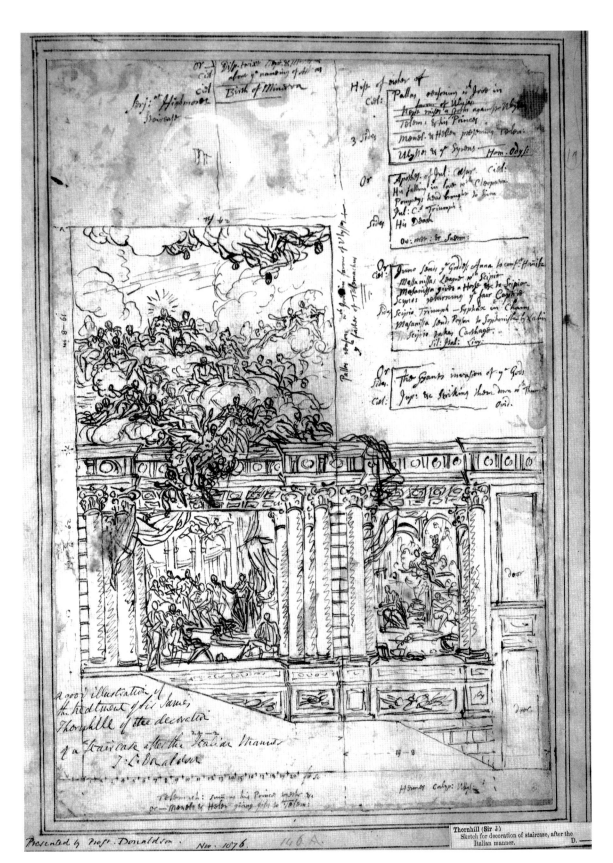

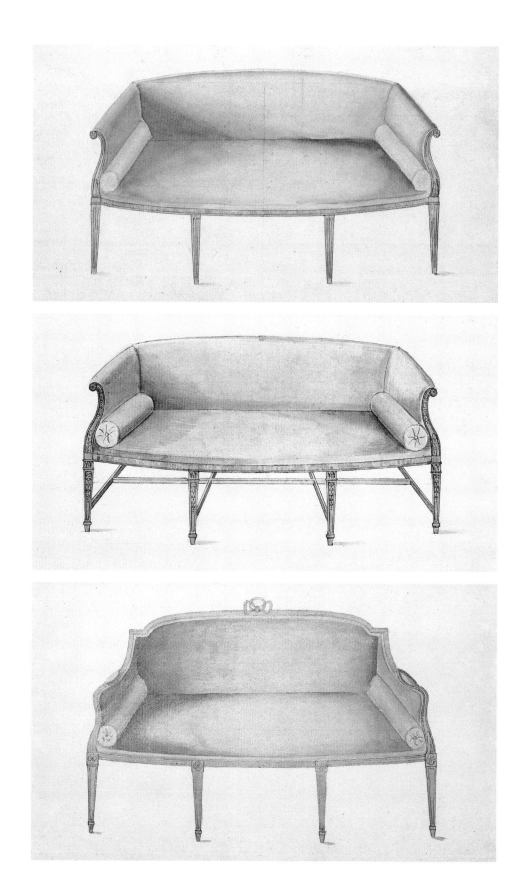

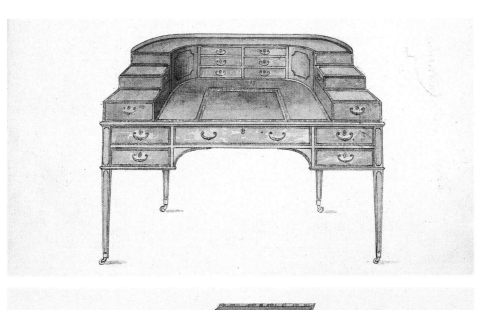

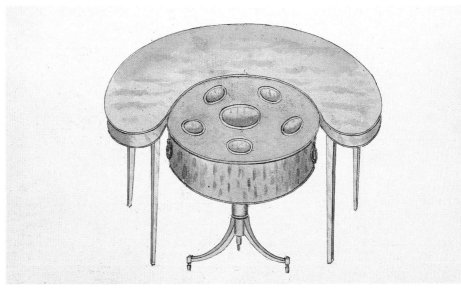

Publishd according to the Act

Wardrobe.

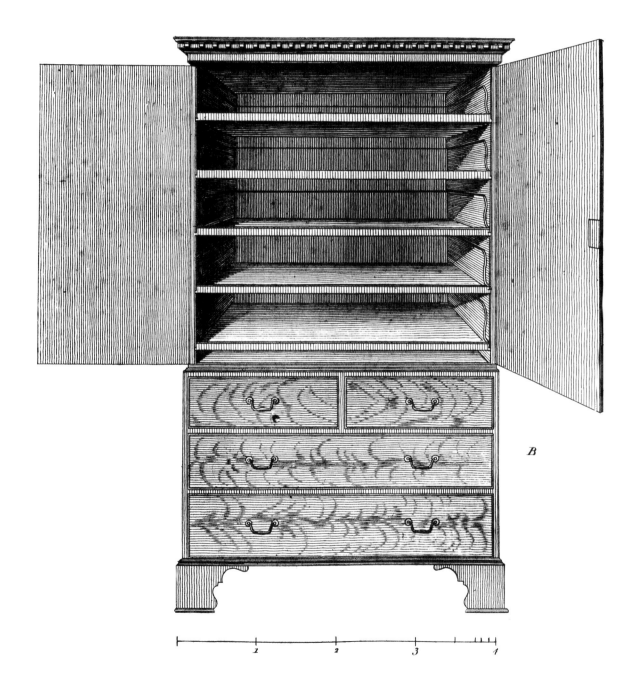

Chests of Drawers

Pub according to Act of Parliam.ᵗ 1753

Elevation of a House for Andrew Millar Esq.
Fronting to Pall Mall

45

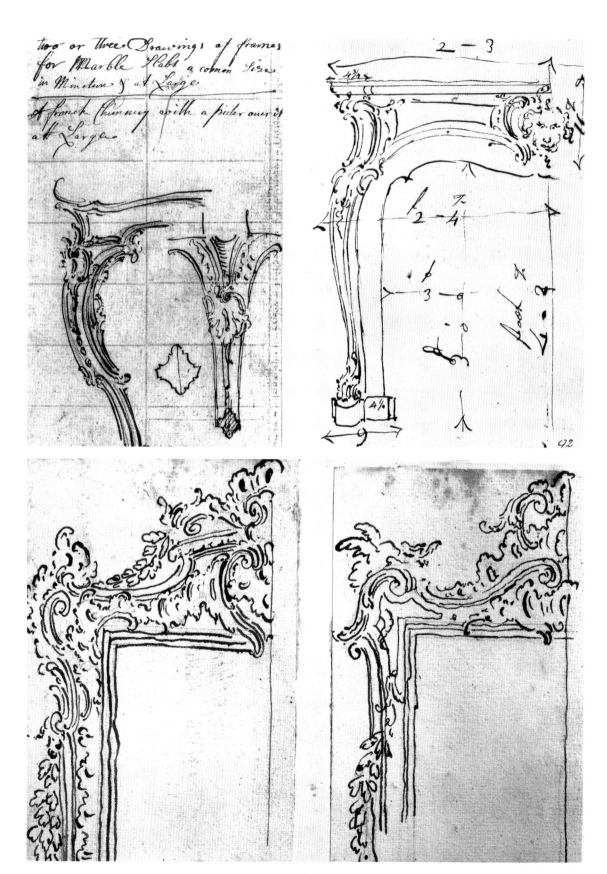

two or three Drawings of frames
for Marble Slabs a common Size
in Miniature & at Large

A french Chimney with a pier over it
at Large

From the West End of Therman Church att Ruen Yeind for a Tabernacle In ye ... Manner Itt being a Comportment

From the Comportment of St Pauls Church Room the West End

Shield with Therlon

My own Desire

The Church of the Virgin Mary att Sorotte an out side Door to the West front

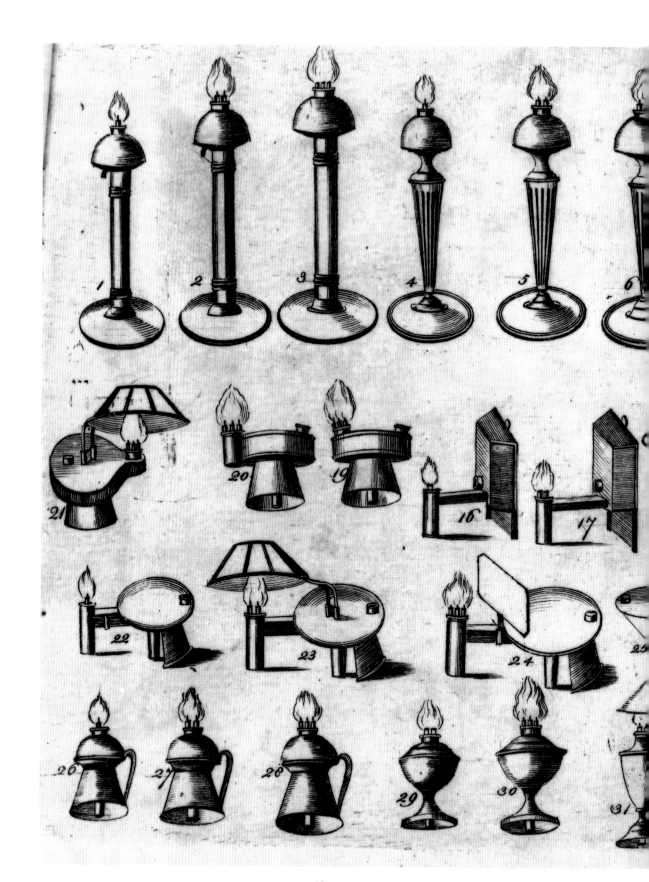

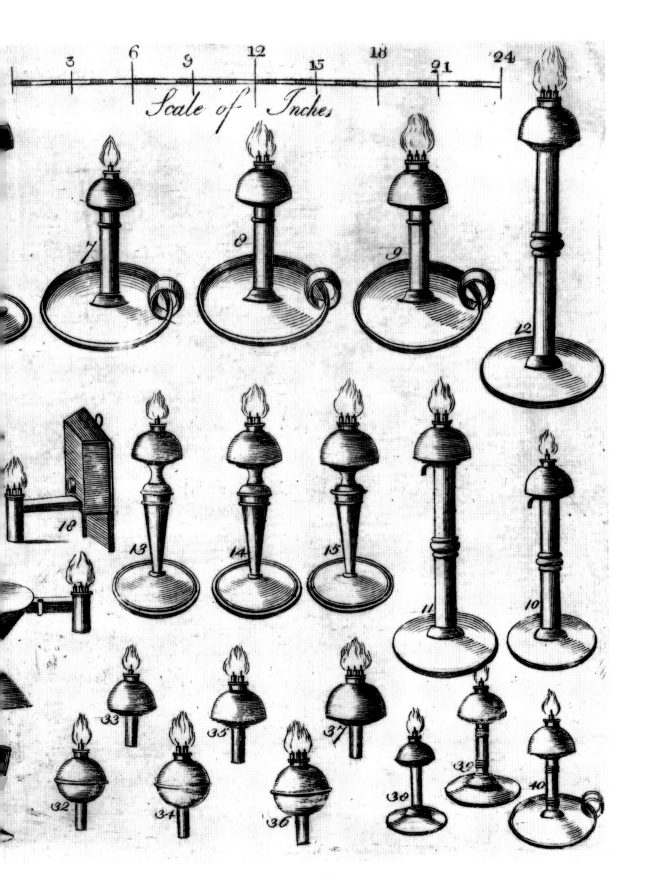

Scale of Inches

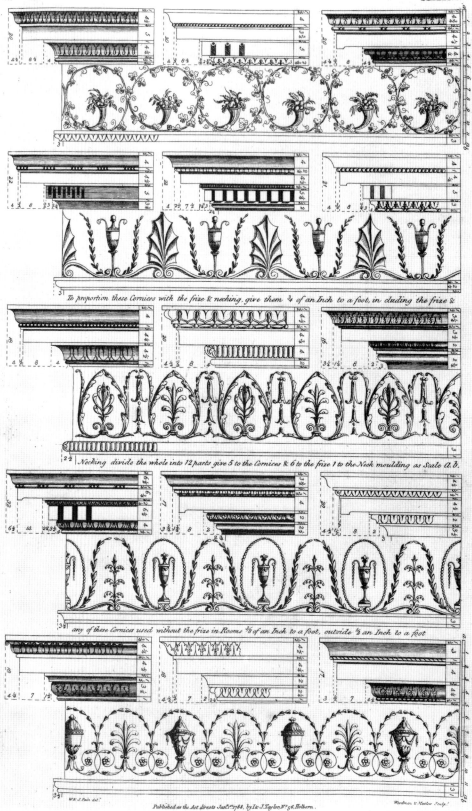

To proportion these Cornices with the frize & necking, give them ¾ of an Inch to a foot, including the frize &

Necking divide the whole into 12 parts give 5 to the Cornices & 6 to the frize 1 to the Neck moulding as Scale A.B.

any of these Cornices used without the frize in Rooms ⅝ of an Inch to a foot, outside ½ an Inch to a foot

W.™ & J.ⁿ Pain del.ᵗ

Published as the Act directs Jan.ʳ 1ˢᵗ 1788, by I.ᵗ J.Taylor, N.º 56, Holborn.

Woodman & Mutlow Sculp.ᵗ

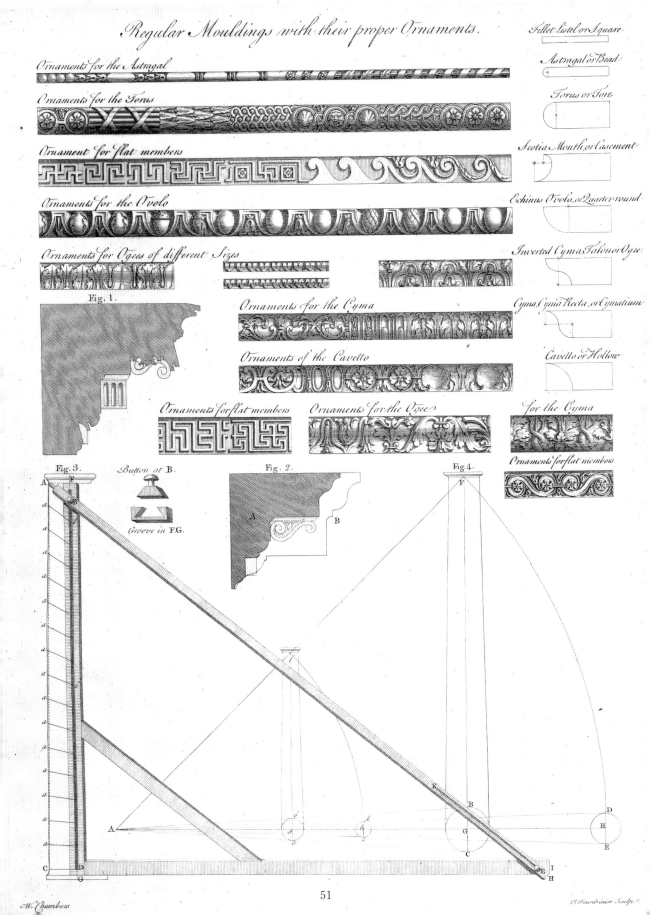

Regular Mouldings with their proper Ornaments.

Fillet Listel or Square

Ornaments for the Astragal

Astragal or Bead

Ornaments for the Torus

Torus or Tore

Ornament for flat members

Scotia Mouth or Casement

Ornaments for the Ovolo

Echinus Ovolo, or Quarter-round

Ornaments for Ogees of different Sizes

Inverted Cyma, Talon or Ogee

Fig. 1.

Ornaments for the Cyma

Cyma, Cyma Recta, or Cymatium

Ornaments of the Cavetto

Cavetto or Hollow

Ornaments for flat members   Ornaments for the Ogee   for the Cyma

Ornaments for flat members

Fig. 3.   Button at B.   Fig. 2.   Fig. 4.

Groove in F.G.

W. Chambers

51

R. Gourdrinier Sculp.

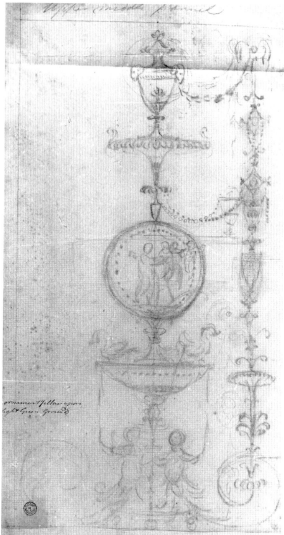

Design for a Toylet Table

J. Chippendale inv.t et delin.   Publish'd according to Act of Parliam.t 1761.   W.t Foster Sculp.

REVIVAL *and* ECLECTICISM

The end of the eighteenth century, then, found English design and decoration very much as it had been during the whole of the century—characterized by a modulated classicism. From metropolitan cabinet-makers to provincial workshops, the dissemination of designs through pattern books had ensured a remarkable homogeneity of style and taste throughout the country. But this situation was not to last for long, as a new eclecticism began to appear. This mixing of styles, which became more noticeable as the new century advanced, has been termed 'the Picturesque'. Initially, it drew on an informed historicism, which grew steadily less authentic as the mid-century approached.

Some of the completed architectural/design schemes – although drawing on a new, exotic repertoire of forms – were remarkably successful. Wyatt's work at Fonthill Abbey, Nash's inspired plans for Brighton Pavilion, and the Sezincote of the Cockerells still displayed a sureness of touch which sprang from the good taste and refined scholarship of the previous generation. But already there was a growing tendency for architects and designers to seek to satisfy the often ill-informed whims of newly rich industrialists and the wealthy merchants and bankers of a rapidly growing middle class.

Yet the beginning of the nineteenth century in the applied arts in England did have a certain look of *status quo*. Sheraton published his *Cabinet Dictionary* in 1803, still expressing the classical ideals of the latter part of the previous century, but with a greater regard for historical authenticity. However, his *Cabinet-maker, Upholsterer and General Artists' Encyclopaedia*, published between 1804 and 1806, shows a number of designs which point to the coming proliferation of styles. He also illustrated several designs with 'Egyptian' motifs, a reflection of the nation's awakened interest in the eastern Mediterranean because of Napoleon's operations there.

I t seems likely, though, that the majority of jobbing craftsmen and designers at the beginning of the nineteenth century still stuck to the well-established classicism of the preceding three decades. There is, for instance, an unassuming purity of line about the variety of patterns for wire fencing, illustrated on p. 69. A notable champion of this surviving classicism was Thomas Hope, who published his *Household Furniture and Interior Decoration* in 1807, essentially as a record of the interiors and furniture of his London house. Classical motifs of chimeras, sphinxes, acanthus leaves and wreaths proliferate in his designs. Hope's interpretation of the antique and its related motifs were taken up by George Smith in his 1808 publication, *Collection of Designs for Household Furniture*.

F rom about 1815, heavier, more florid forms begin to appear in English design. It is hard to know quite why this came about, but it is worth noting that the end of the Napoleonic wars offered greater travel opportunities to wealthy Englishmen who, in turn, developed a liking of the heavy French Empire style. In furniture making, brass inlay became popular, especially in floral and grotesque patterns which, in the worst cases, swamped whole areas of any piece. In other words, the Regency period saw a movement in English design from the supreme elegance of the Sheraton era to a coarseness which we normally associate with the Victorian period which follows. Furniture designs look over-ornate and even simple household objects begin to look too elaborate for their function.

page 56 The Spode factory flourished in the early nineteenth century under the founder's son Josiah II (1754-1827), producing a variety of transfer-printed wares with designs of classical and Oriental scenes. This page from a print record book of 1806 shows a variety of border patterns and Greek centres. These were printed from copper plates in black or brown in the record book, but were actually used on Spode china and porcelain in dark blue. The final pages of this book contain the record of the badges, crests and back stamps used on special orders or for individual customers.

right Hand-block printing of calico in an early nineteenth-century workshop; this illustration is taken from *The Book of English Trades Part III* (1805) by R. Phillips.

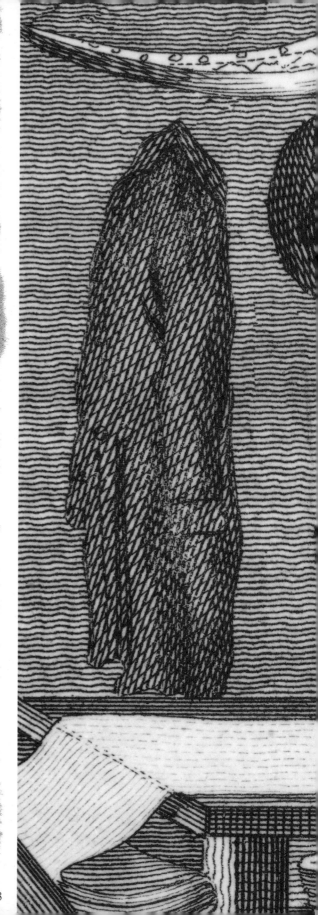

2

REVIVAL
and
ECLECTICISM

pages 60–61

Thomas Hope (1769-1831) published his *Household Furniture and Interior Decoration* in 1807, chiefly as a record of the interiors of his London home. He designed furniture in the Greek and Egyptian styles to accompany his collections of antiquities. His Egyptian furniture (the 'Egyptian room' is illustrated here), especially, provided models for other cabinet-makers, already inspired by the nation's military and naval interests in the eastern Mediterranean. His influence on English furniture design was considerable, and sphinxes, lions and hieroglyphics now became part of the national design vocabulary.

page 65

The firm of Gillow (see pp. 38-39) was especially prolific in its designs during the late Georgian and Regency period. This design for a lady's dressing-table, for instance, is one of a series produced around the turn of the century. Other versions included one in the style of a desk and a rounded design with lift-up lid. These were entered as pencil sketches in the company's record books, complete with dimensions.

pages 66–67

This design for a *faux* bamboo sofa appears in a Gillow sketchbook of designs dating from the very end of the 18th century. It reflects the continuing taste for Oriental artefacts and would probably have been made from a local wood painted to resemble bamboo. A chair of similar design, made in beech, has been precisely dated to 1794. Gillow's continuing success was almost certainly due to the firm's policy of making attractive, affordable furniture in a wide range of forms which appealed to a burgeoning urban middle class.

page 68

Four pages from *The London Chairmakers' and Carvers' Book of Prices for Workmanship*; the prefatory pages of this volume, dated 1807, note that there is an introduction by R.J. Adam 'as regulated and agreed to by a committee of master chair manufacturers and journeymen, with methods of computation adopted in the work, illustrated by reference to a variety of figures, engraved on sixteen copper plates.'

page 69

The persistence of classical inspiration in design in the early nineteenth century is abundantly evident in the architect L.N. Cottingham's *Smith and Founder's Director* of 1823 (2nd edition 1824) which illustrated a multiplicity of designs for railings and balconies; these would then have been copied by foundries at the request of builders and architects. The volume, indeed, was described as 'a director containing a series of designs and patterns for ornamental iron and brass work.' The introduction to the book concludes with the hope that the work will 'remove in some measure the severe and painful regret that has long been felt by ingenious workmen, for the want of a collection of good ornaments to select from, at a price within the compass of their limited means…' The 'several hundred specimens' are chosen from 'the choicest productions of the Grecian, Etruscan, Roman and Gothic schools…'

pages 70–71

It was common practice for textile mills to maintain records of production in the form of swatch books, in which tiny samples of the printed fabric would be mounted after manufacture, occasionally juxtaposed with the original painted design. These pages are reproduced from a swatch book of the Rossendale Printing Company, whose factory was in the Rossendale valley, close to Manchester. The book covers the years 1815-20 and contains 216 pages with 24 printed cotton swatches on each side in a variety of plain and patterned designs printed in shades of rust, yellow, dark red, blue, pink and green.

pages 72–73

Ever ingenious, the manufacturers of Sheffield plate and silver had, by the early nineteenth century, begun to offer a bewildering variety of household utensils to a gadget-conscious and status-seeking middle class. These designs of egg-cup holders are taken from an unidentified manufacturer's pattern book of *c*. 1825, offering candlesticks, candelabra, snuffers, epergnes,

REVIVAL
and
ECLECTICISM

cruet sets, ink stands, wine funnels, coasters, toast-racks, meat dishes and covers, and tea and coffee pots in 127 engraved plates.

pages 74–75

Founded by Josiah Wedgwood at Burslem, Staffordshire, in 1759, Wedgwood has remained one of the pre-eminent English potteries. Its first generations of wares closely reflected the prevailing Neoclassicism of the latter part of the 18th century, incorporating motifs from the statuary, plaques, urns and vases of antiquity. The pottery became especially famous for its jasperware which was characterized by white decorative motifs of classical inspiration on a blue or greenish ground. Even for the decoration of utilitarian wares, such as the teapots illustrated here, the pottery employed artists of note, including George Stubbs and John Flaxman. The range of wares produced by the factory – known as Etruria – was extensive, as the entries in the company records show. These teapot samples, drawn from the Shapes Number One Book, a

record book begun in the 18th century which catalogues both ornamental and utilitarian pieces, includes both late eighteenth- and nineteenth-century models.

pages 76–77

This illustration of a soup tureen is drawn from the same pattern book as that described in the caption to pp. 72-73. The manufacturer's concern to offer a multiplicity of choice to his customers is evident in the ingenious device of illustrating two different forms of decoration on one shape. The manufacturer further noted in his introductory remarks that the wares on offer had been drawn on a scale of six inches to the foot. The silver circles on some designs denote the placement for silver crests, while the figure of a hand indicates silver mountings.

pages 78–79

Carpet factories have existed in Kidderminster, south-west of Birmingham, since the early 17th century, but it was the first decades of the nineteenth century which saw

a major expansion of the industry in the town. Between 1807 and 1838 the number of looms in operation increased from one thousand to over two thousand. These designs are taken from the archive of Woodward Grosvenor, founded in 1790 and still in existence today. They all date from *c.* 1800, incorporating five or six colours in designs by anonymous artists.

page 80

These designs for lace are taken from a 106-page sketch book now in the possession of the Victoria & Albert Museum, London. The fly-leaf bears the name of Isabel Haddon Odiham, although there is no suggestion that she was the actual designer; the characteristics of the paper suggest that the book dates from between 1809 and 1820. The pages are filled with designs for borders and larger patterns, some of which are extended to fold-outs.

page 81

Another design from the archives of Woodward Grosvenor, Kidderminster;

prior to 1905, the company's designs were painted in miniature to half or a third scale to save expensive paper. This pattern for a hearth rug is in 13 colours and would have been mirrored in the other three quarters of the piece to complete the design.

page 82

Executed between 1809 and 1820, these designs for toast-racks are taken from three narrow pages of a pattern book recording the designs of Edward Barnard & Sons, manufacturing silversmiths. The first Edward Barnard set up a business partnership in 1808, after working for Thomas Chawner from 1773, becoming Edward Barnard & Sons in 1829 and moving to a new factory in the City of London in 1830. The company continues in existence as a subsidiary of Padgett & Braham Ltd. Now lodged in the collection of the Victoria & Albert Museum, London, the company archive comprises some 250 ledger volumes containing records from its inception to 1961. The production orders of the company record such eminent clients as Elkington & Co. and Garrard's.

2

REVIVAL
and
ECLECTICISM

page 83

This 5-colour 'Strawberries' design, half of a 27-inch pattern, among the many thousands in the archive of Woodward Grosvenor, is typical in its anonymity. Unsigned, only a code number enables dating to be done with any accuracy. But in this lies its significance: a national design archive consists of so much more than the well-publicized works of a few familiar names. Woodward Grosvenor undertakes special commissions to manufacture carpets to designs in its archve, which computerization has made immediately accessible.

pages 84–85

These elegant designs, meticulously drawn in pen and ink by an anonymous hand, are the records for mugs and pots to be made as cream ware, lead-glazed pottery with a flint content which resulted in a cream-coloured body. The pottery producing these designs is no longer known, although each pattern has a production number. Geometric decoration would have been applied mechanically with an engine-powered lathe, the floral elements being added as transfers.

pages 86–87

These leaves from an album of designs for ceramic wares lodged in the collection of the Victoria & Albert Museum, London, are further testimony to the vision of the anonymous craftsmen who created them. Utilitarian yet elegant, the designs are drawn directly on to the pages of well-worn calf-bound volumes, believed to be the record of the production of Messrs. Hartley Greens & Co. One of the volumes is stamped with the words 'New Teapot Book'.

pages 88–89

Like the ceramic designs on the preceding pages, these textile designs provide even more evidence of the wealth of design talent employed in the workshops and factories of early nineteenth-century England. Reproduced from a 299-page volume now in the Victoria & Albert Museum, London; each page bears between eight and ten immaculately conceived and executed designs, each grouping positioned symmetrically on the page.

pages 90–95

These pages are taken, like the illustrations on pp. 86-87, from the set of albums in the collection of the Victoria & Albert Museum, London, believed to be the production records of Messrs. Hartley Greens & Co. One album, containing the records of jugs and tureens (pp. 90-91), is made up of sheets of grid paper on which are pasted finely detailed pen and wash drawings. The date 18 February 1802 appears inside the front cover. Another album (pp. 92-95) bears the legend 'Original Drawing Book No. 1' on its glazed brown cardboard cover. The designs are either separately mounted or drawn directly on to the pages of bluish paper, accompanied with descriptive notes of range variations and code numbers.

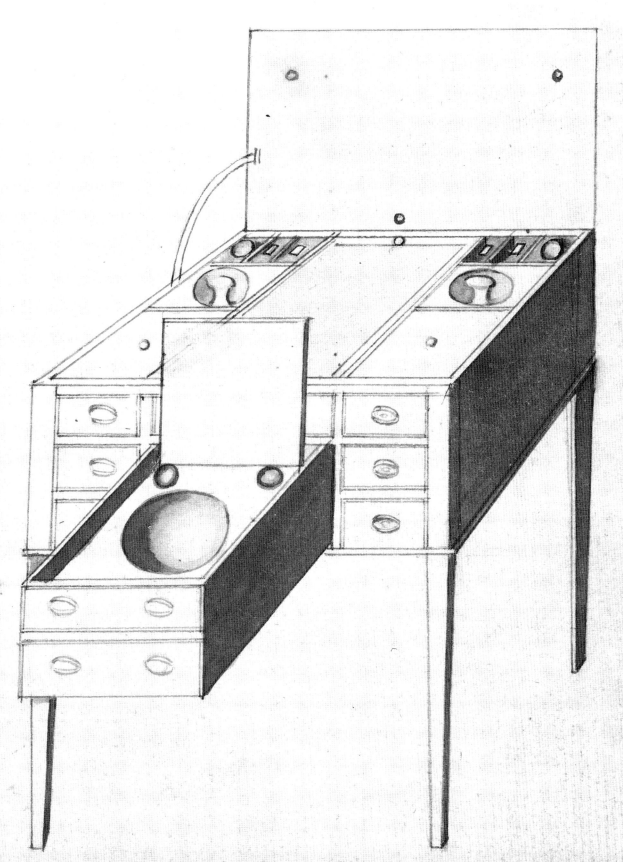

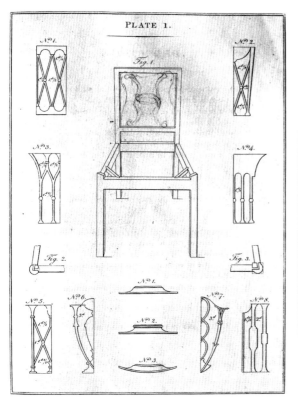

PLATE 1.

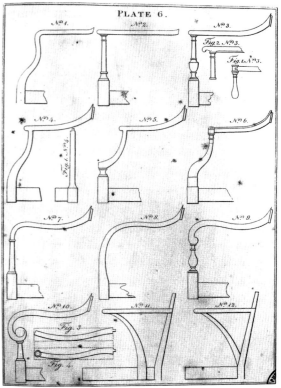

PLATE 6.

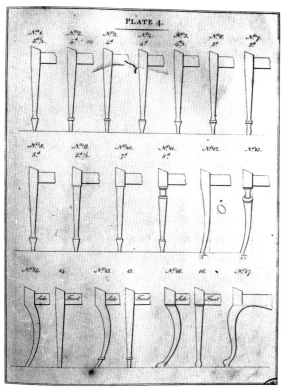

PLATE 4.

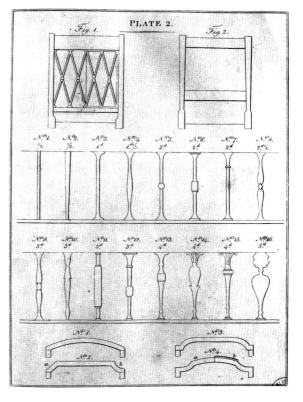

PLATE 2.

PLATE XVII

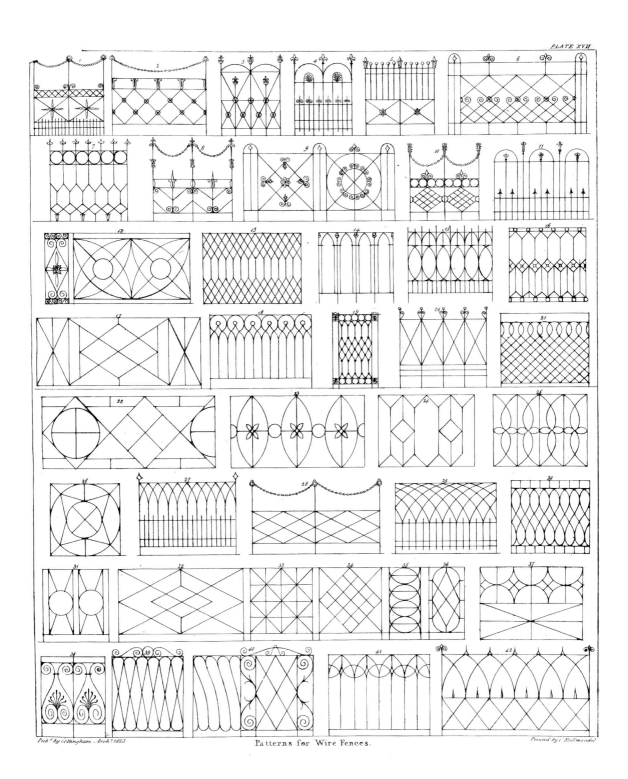

Pub.^d by Cottingham . Arch.^t 1823

Patterns for Wire Fences.

Printed by C. Hullmandel

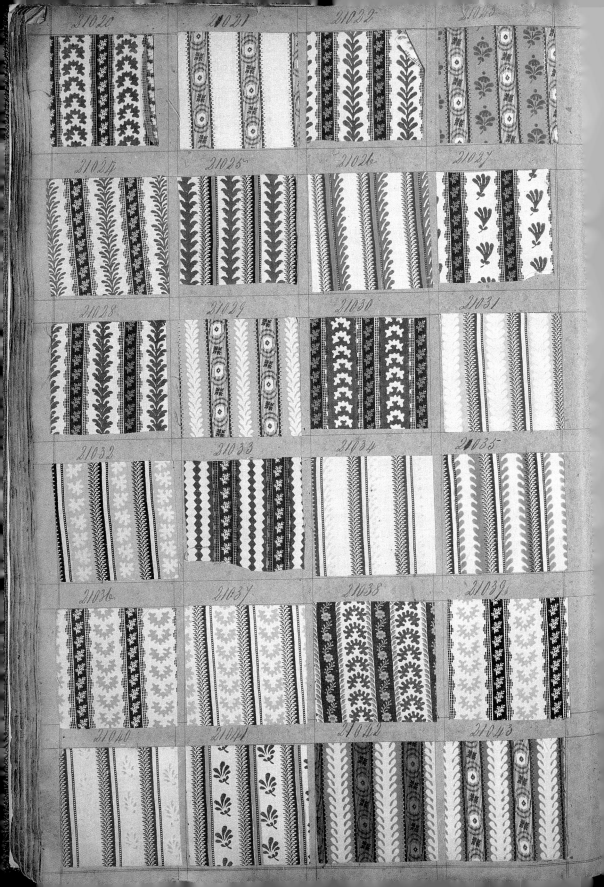

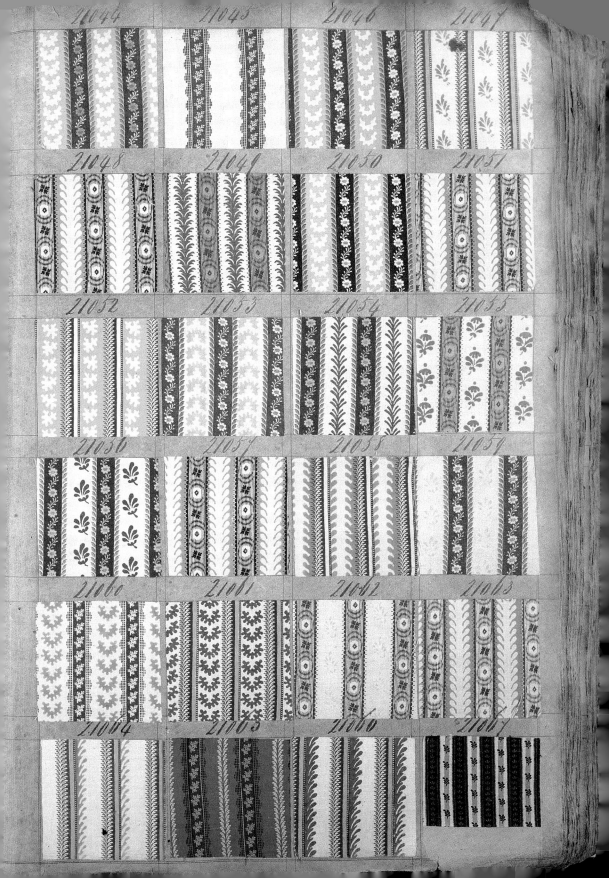

21044 21045 21046 21047
21048 21049 21050 21051
21052 21053 21054 21055
21056 21057 21058 21059
21060 21061 21062 21063
21064 21065 21066 21067

164

3001

Sauce

163

o match

130 Cords by 280 Lashes — to drop 278 140 Lashes

Point d'oose 132 by 240

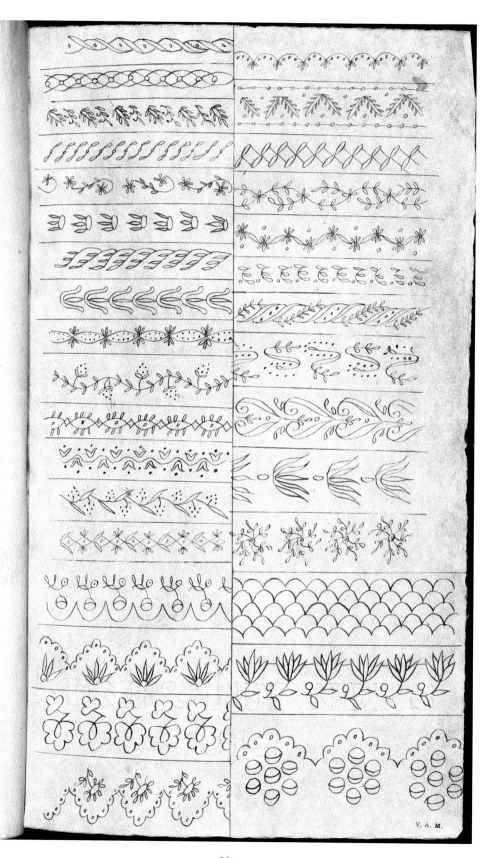

V.A.M.

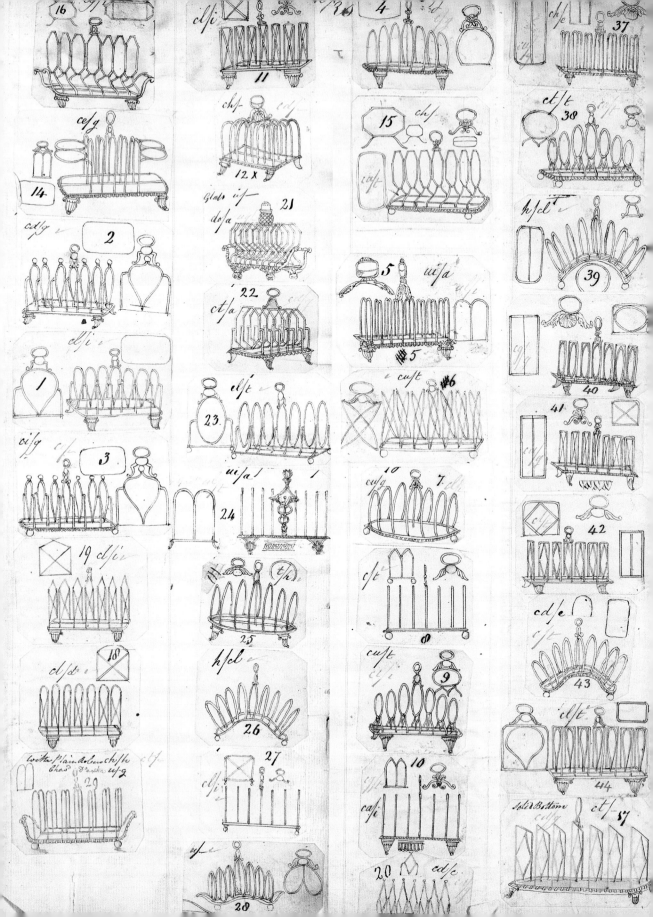

136 by 160
83
bottom

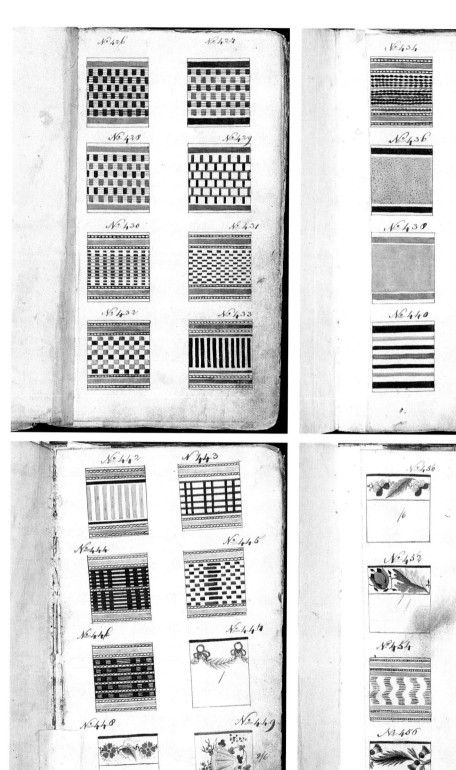

No 346

Dip

347

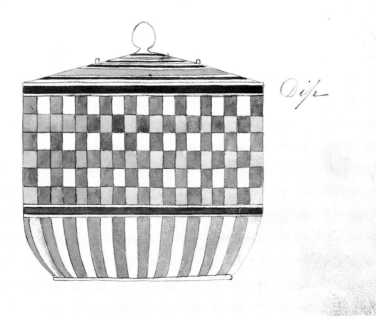

Dip

No. 376

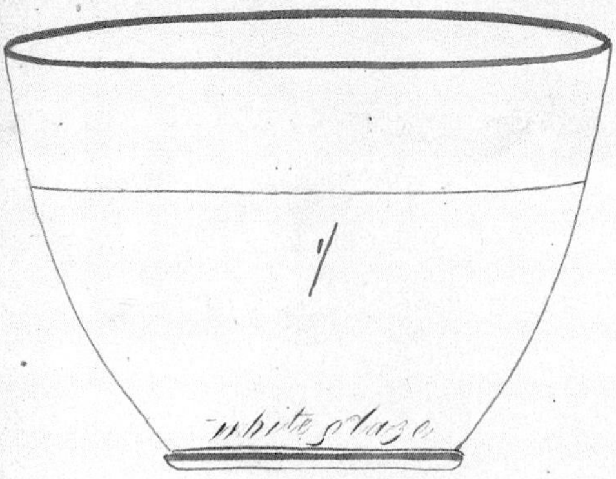

No. 377

1

1

white glaze

white glaze

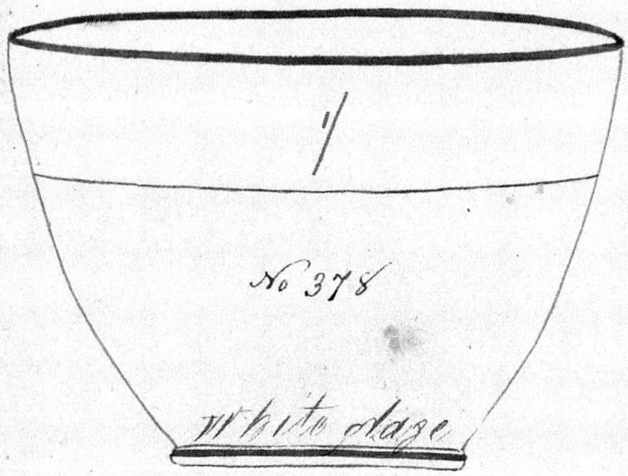

1

1

No. 378

No. 379

white glaze

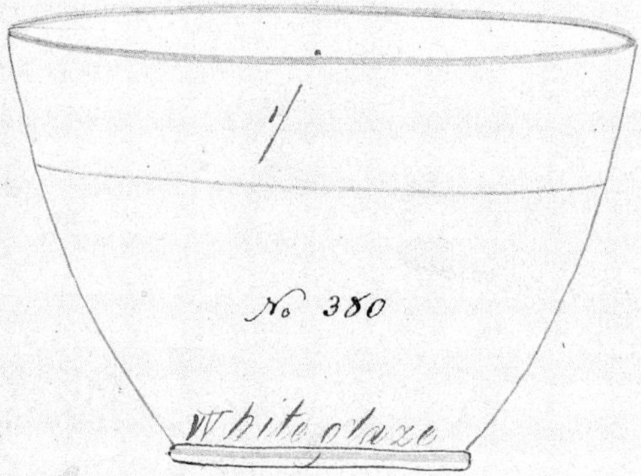

white glaze

1

1/6

No. 380

No. 381

White glaze

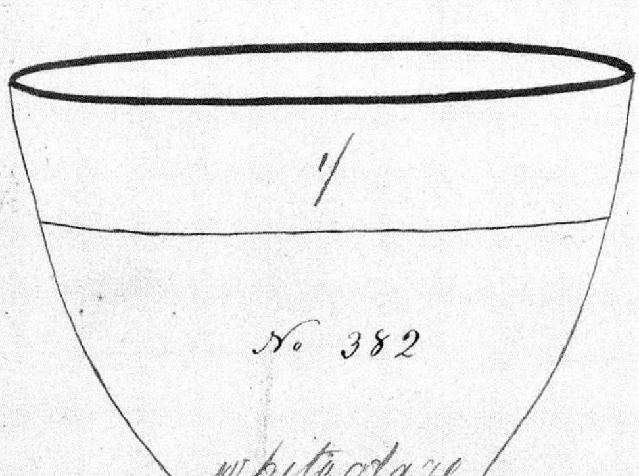

white glaze

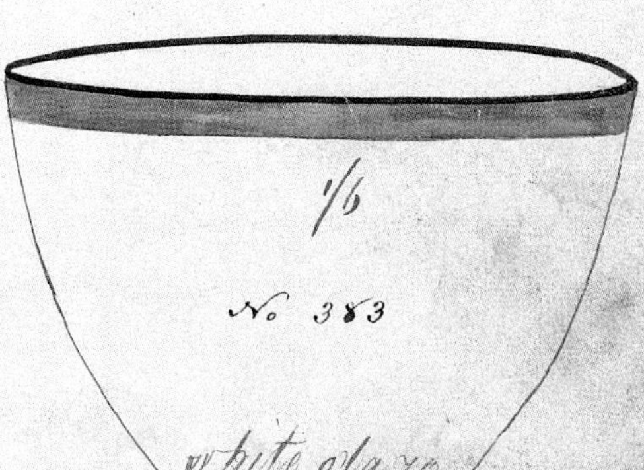

1

1/6

No. 382

No. 383

white glaze

white glaze

No 384   1/6

white glaze

No 385   1/6

white glaze

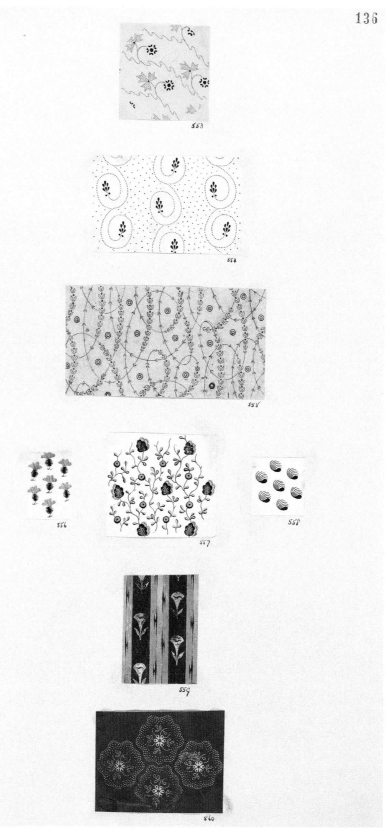

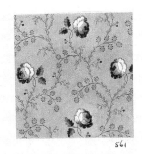

561

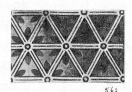

562

563

564

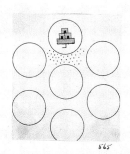

565

566

567

568

I.V. 18th febry 1802

N° 1.

N° 2. N° 3.

N° 4. N° 5.

N° 6. 12

N° 7.

N° 8. 14

V.A.M.

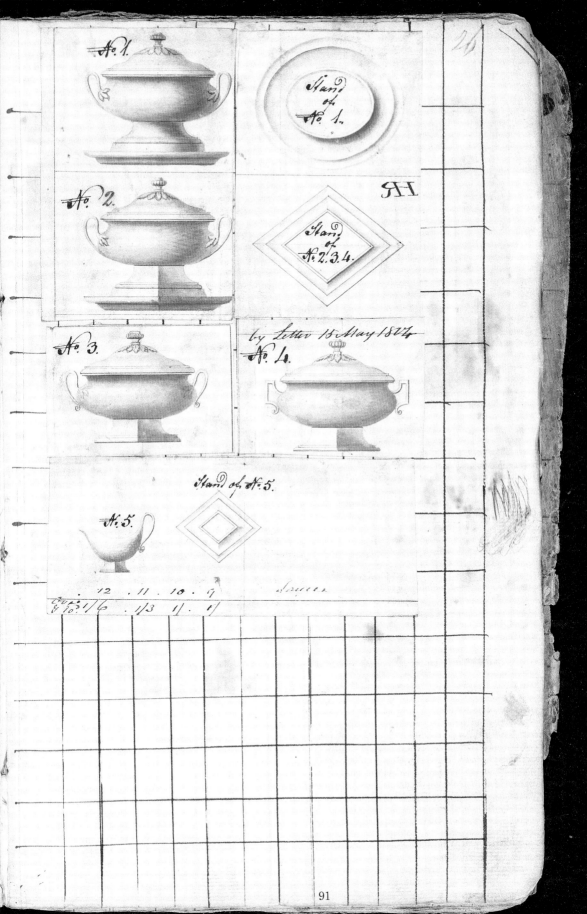

Nº 1.

Stand
of
Nº 1.

Nº 2.

ℛℋ

Stand
of
Nº 2. 3. 4.

Nº 3.

by Letter 15 May 1824
Nº 4.

Stand of Nº 5.

Nº 5.

	12	11	10	9	Saucer
ℰ to 1/6		1/3	1/	1/	

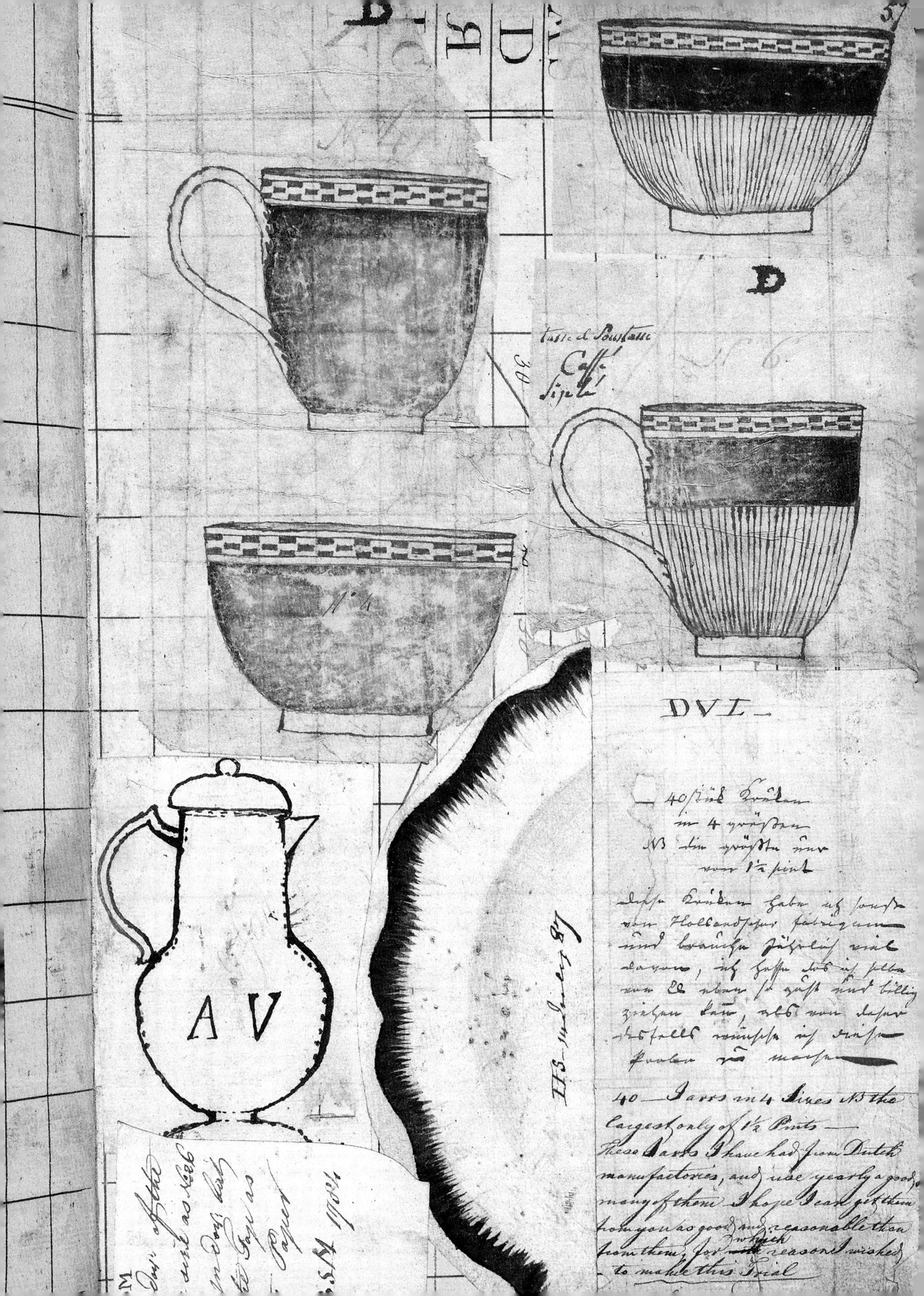

D

tasse à pousse tasse
Caffé
Tasse

N° 6

N° 4

D V L —

40 Jars in 4 sizes NB the largest only of 1½ Pints —
These Jars I have had from Dutch manufactories, and use yearly a good many of them I hope I can get them from you as good and reasonable than from them, for which reason I wished to make this Trial

N.1.

N.2.

N.3.

N.4.

made of the White Cake

made of the Glaze of the same ware

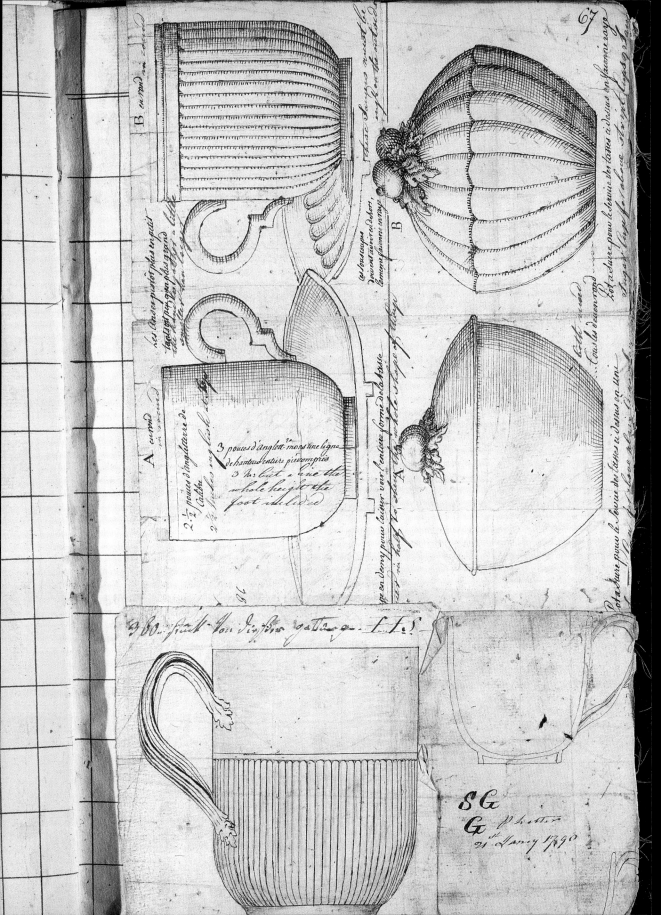

67

B en rond

Les tasses piedot plus vuide

A en rond

3 pouces d'anglet. moins une ligne
de hauteur entire peu compris
3 In but a une the
whole height the
foot included

2.½ pouces d'angleterre de
Caliba

2¾ inches in bodt the thige

qui en demy pour hauteur vui l'entiere forme de la tasse
the whole shape the tasse

A

B

SG
G. P....
21 Jan. 1790

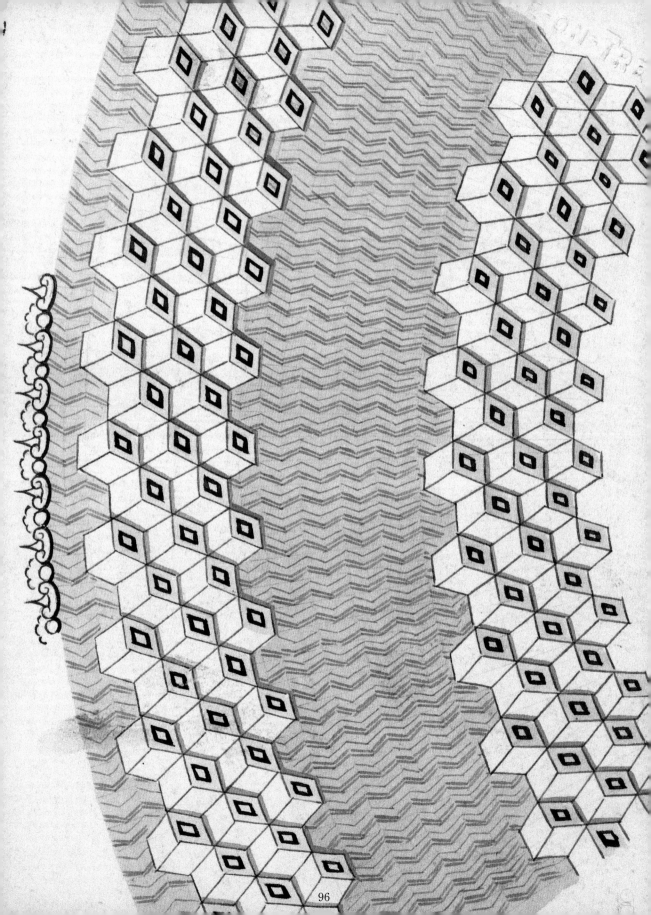

Early Victorian

the
ORKSHOP
OF THE WORLD

The years between 1830 and 1851 saw England assume a position of apparent unassailability in world manufacturing and economic affairs. Yet the factors which ensured this pre-eminence – the growth of a factory culture and its related financial structure – also had an unfortunate effect on English design. The largely classical heritage which had survived reasonably intact into the early years of the century had been dissipated by 1830, as patronage passed from an informed and well-travelled aristocracy and upper middle class to a middle class whose taste was formed essentially by the manufacturers whose wares it bought in profusion. It was as though there was simply not enough good design to go round, as factories and workshops turned out goods in a bewildering variety of styles, often in inappropriately elaborate and exaggerated forms, perceived as the chief means of seeing off the competition.

The paucity of good English design in this period was made only too evident by the Great Exhibition of 1851, where far too many exhibits seemed preoccupied with the grotesque and vulgar detail of a half-understood traditionalism. After the exhibition, the tide of criticism of English design of the early and mid Victorian periods continued unabated until well into the twentieth century. The great Victorian reforming designers, from Burges and Morris to the major figures of the Arts and Crafts Movement, deliberately reacted against it; later critics, guided by an aesthetic formed by the precepts of the early Modern Movement, regarded its wild excesses almost as a manifestation of absolute evil. And we can see in the pages which follow that there is enough evidence of the tendency to disregard rightness of form for function in favour of crude visual effect: in wallpaper design, in interior design, in the styling of simple domestic artefacts.

The unsatisfactory appearance of much design of the period undoubtedly came from its eclecticism: there was virtually nothing in the way of new forms, just aspects of past styles, sometimes thrown together in the same artefact or pattern. Yet this same eclecticism, notably in furniture, did occasionally result in effective and pleasing pieces.

any of the stylistic devices of the time were undoubtedly affected by the prevailing mood of national self-confidence in their derivation from a specifically English past. 'Tudor', 'Elizabethan' and 'Jacobean' interiors were considered most appropriate to the many new country houses built in the first half of the nineteenth century. 'Elizabethan' was one of the styles considered by a Parliamentary Select Committee in 1835 for the design of the future Palace of Westminster. Again, printed pattern books were instrumental in the dissemination of styles, except that now such books would be used by mass-manufacturers as well as individual craftsmen. As we have noted in the general introduction, Robert Bridgens' *Furniture with Candelabra and Interior Decoration* of 1838 makes 'Elizabethan' its most extensive category of design.

lmost as important in Bridgens' book is the 'Grecian' category, which was effectively a continuation of Regency classicism. However, a new clumsiness had invaded the pure, elegant forms of the late eighteenth and early nineteenth centuries. Notable among the manufacturers of late 'Regency' was the firm of Gillow – a name which will recur throughout English nineteenth-century design as an indicator of popular taste.

The other style – eventually chosen – under consideration by the 1835 Committee on Westminster was 'Gothic'. Although it had still yielded pride of place to a gradually debased classicism in the early years of the century, in spite of isolated successful examples of Regency 'Gothick', Gothic was seen as another national, nordic style, as opposed to Mediterranean classicism. But typically of an age as contradictory and complex as the early Victorian, manufacturers and designers still frequently turned to Louis Quinze Rococo and to classical models for inspiration.

The Gothic style had an additional role, however, which gave it an importance well beyond its presence as part of the Regency and early Victorian design mix. It was also a vehicle for the first stirrings of design reform, providing a repertoire of motifs and forms which ran counter to the fussy, vulgar detailing of mainstream manufactured artefacts.

he first significant reformer to deploy this visual vocabulary and its related values was Augustus Welby Pugin whose two publications, *Gothic Furniture* and *The True Principles of Printed or Christian Architecture*, set forth new tenets of design responsibility in materials and form: '…there should be no features about a building which are not necessary for convenience, construction or propriety… all ornament should consist of enrichment of the essential construction of the building.' In his furniture, although by no means wholly consistent, Pugin veered away from the decorative tracery of Regency 'Gothick' towards an 'authentic', simplified style of Gothic which drew heavily on concepts of the medieval. The results have a toughness and honesty which point forward to the works of the later Victorian reformers.

ther voices were raised against the prevailing manufacturers' aesthetic, notably those of Henry Cole, Owen Jones and Matthew Digby Wyatt. In 1849 Cole launched on important publication, *The Journal of Design and Manufacture*, which based its editorial policy on the principle that, 'Ornament… must be secondary to the thing decorated.' But the century had a very long way to go before such principles could be applied to any significant degree in the manufacturing industry of Victorian England. Perhaps the most positive aspect of this period of English design is indeed its exuberance and energy, its sheer volume; and there are, in any case, many examples of intrinsic interest and great ingenuity, demonstrating a conscious effort by certain companies and individuals to apply a responsible design ethic to manufacture.

page 96 Pen and ink design of ceramic wares, for the Derby Crown Porcelain Company, from the originals now held in the Victoria & Albert Museum, London.

opposite Scenes from an early nineteenth-century pottery factory; the biscuit kiln would have been used for the production of an unglazed white porcelain, often used in the making of statuettes and other decorative objects.

VARIOUS POTTERY PROCESSES.

1. THE "THROWER."

2. THE "TURNER."

3. THE "BISCUIT OVEN."

4. PRINTING.

5. ORNAMENTING.

3

THE WORKSHOP
of the
WORLD

Traditionalism and eclecticism: the library at Cassiobury, Essex, *c.* 1830, from an aquatint by F. Lewis based on a drawing by Augustus Pugin, published in 1837. The Fifth Earl of Essex, who succeeded to the title in 1799, commissioned James Wyatt to modify the Restoration house in the Gothick style.

The archive of Wycombe Museum, at the centre of England's traditional furniture-making region, contains fascinating material relating to the vernacular styles of the nineteenth century. These designs, in the form of small gouache paintings, appeared in a catalogue attributed to Walter Skull, furniture-maker. Each of the volume's 170 pages bears three separate designs, some with prices, as though this material was originally intended for the use of a salesman.

The Whitefriars glassworks, originally located between Fleet Street and the river Thames in London, had been in existence for well over a century when James Powell took over its management in 1835. It then became a leader in the revival of English hand-blown glass-making, promoting designs derived from Roman, Venetian, medieval and eighteenth-century models. The earliest Whitefriars pattern book, now in the Museum of London, contains 495 pages of hand-drawn designs, many of them dating from the 1830s. Most of these are for tableware, often annotated with prices and customer names. Shapes include claret jugs and bottles, some intricately engraved and with rope-ring finials, as well as glasses in all forms, such as those illustrated here.

In 1833 the Spode pottery and porcelain factory was taken over by W.T. Copeland, a partner since 1813 and in charge of the London showroom, and Thomas Garrett, who became the partner to manage the Staffordshire end of the business. The contemporary revival of interest in the art of Ancient Greece is reflected in this 1833 design for an earthenware water ewer, decorated with whimsical Greek figures on a salmon-coloured ground. The ewer was part of a set which included a two-handled vase and a teacup which are illustrated on the opposite page of a master pattern book in the Spode Museum Trust.

This crowded sheet of designs for glassware *c.* 1840 by Leopold William Jones is a concentrated demonstration of how traditionalist and revivalist styles began to assume varied and exaggerated forms as the mid-century approached. Classical forms are here overblown in a disregard for rightness of form and a fondness for crude visual effect.

Shoolbred, Loveridge & Shoolbred of Wolverhampton described themselves as makers of paper and Japan tea trays, general japanners, and iron and tin-plate workers. This company – located in one of England's industrial heartlands – was very much the epitome of the expansive Victorian business catering for the ever-growing market in domestic products of variable design excellence. These designs for the company's jelly and blancmange moulds are taken from a catalogue of 1847, the introduction to which begs to remind customers that the wares on offer 'can only be shown as regards ornament, through the medium of patterns.'

These two pages of teacup designs are taken from a master Spode pattern book containing, in all, 1,432 different patterns. Each of the designs is numbered and can be collated with the actual production records of the factory. All the cups illustrated here were to be made in bone china and date from the years just prior to the takeover of the factory by W.T. Copeland.

This selection of doorknobs and fastenings appears in a 340-page catalogue of engraved products manufactured by J. Rimmell & Sons. It is yet another demonstration of the colossal variety of forms and shapes

3

THE WORKSHOP
of the
WORLD

available to the mid-Victorian market, when labour was cheap and the housing market in full expansion. The first page of the catalogue offers 'patterns priced etc. of Sheffield brass etc., furniture, fittings, domestic utensils.'

page 115

Another anonymous pattern book held by the Victoria & Albert Museum contains 145 pages of designs for light accessories and other metal fittings. These include candlesticks, as illustrated here, candelabra, hanging and standing lamps, as well as desk furniture, including letter-racks and ink-wells.

pages 116–117

During the 1840s the number of looms in the carpet-manufacturing centre of Kidderminster increased to more than 3,000 (see caption to pp. 78-79). For once anonymity seems to have been ignored and this original gouache painting is inscribed on the back, 'Edward Poole, designer of Kidderminster'. The design of banana leaves (p. 116) would have been woven on a Wilton loom *c.* 1830. The design on p.

117 was for a 27-inch half-drop pattern with a repeat at approximately 40 inches. The 11-colour design, painted in miniature, is dated 1830 on the back and would, again, have been woven on a Wilton loom.

pages 118–119

These designs, for the Derby Crown Porcelain Co. Ltd., are part of a book of ceramic patterns now held in the Victoria & Albert Museum, London. Each pattern, meticulously drawn in pen and ink, is accompanied by a company name and code number. The designs were clearly intended to be the original artwork for transfers. Porcelain factories had flourished in Derby from the mid 18th century; indeed, the town became known as 'the second Dresden'.

pages 120–121

Samples for wallpaper borders drawn from a precisely annotated album, dated 1840-41; again, the sheer variety of design on offer to the domestic decoration market of mid-Victorian England is astounding. It is perhaps small wonder that, given the sheer

volume of production, it sometimes seemed as though there was not enough good design to go round, and artists often worked for a number of different factories.

pages 122–123

Two further examples of design from the Rossendale Printing Co. (see pp. 70-71); the page illustrated on p. 122 dates from the early 1830s and shows samples of printed cottons. The complete book consists of 184 pages with engraved roller-printed and block print floral designs densely applied to each side. The swatch book of printed cottons, from which a page is reproduced on p. 123, is later in date (*c.* 1850). It consists of 234 pages with a variety of printed cotton swatches applied to each side in patterned, shaded and moiré-effect designs.

pages 124–125

The documentation accompanying this Rococo-inspired design for a Woodward Grosvenor carpet is more complete than is usually the case. Firstly, it is meticulously dated on the back: 18 September 1847. It is

also known that it was executed by the studio of the designer Anna Maria Garthwaite, who provided hundreds of designs for Woodward Grosvenor. It was sent, simply rolled and without protection, through the post (there is a Penny Red stamp on the back) to a Mrs Pardoe. The complex design uses 13 colours and would have been woven as a 27-inch Wilton.

page 126

Among the many pattern books in the Spode Museum Trust are six devoted to tile design. The Number Two Book, from which these designs are taken, contains 155 hand-painted patterns on paper, pasted down on to the actual pages of the book. Most of the designs are in a square format, although there are a very small number of rounded shapes.

page 127

A decorative adjunct to England's growing industrial might: a watercolour design for the ceiling of the refreshment room of Swindon station; this intricate pattern was designed in 1842 by F.&T. Grace.

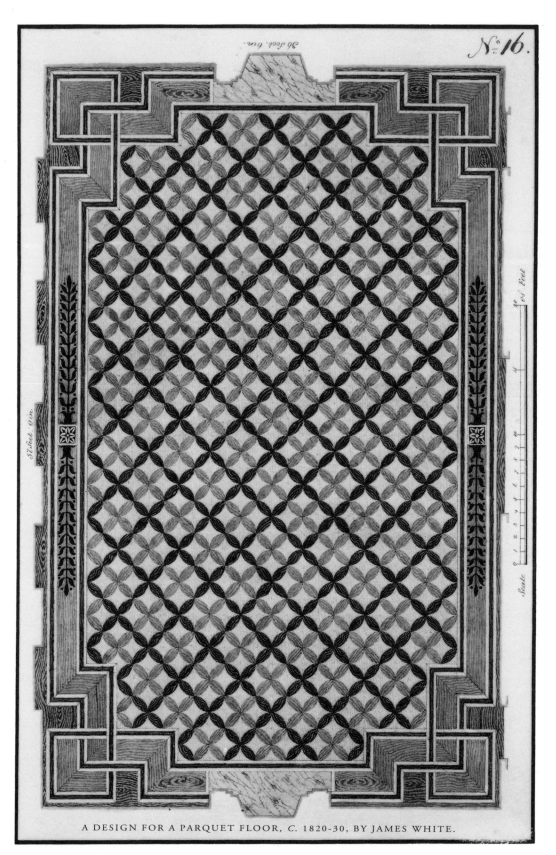

A DESIGN FOR A PARQUET FLOOR, *C.* 1820-30, BY JAMES WHITE.

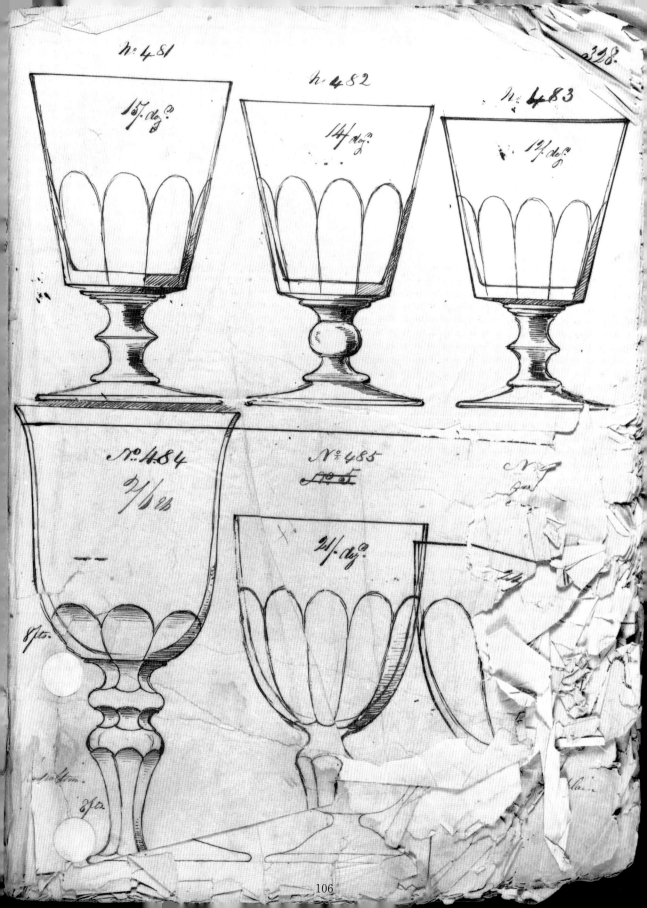

N.º 481

15/ doz.º

N. 482

14/ doz.º

N. 483

13/ doz.º

328.

N.º 484

2/6 Zb

N.º 485

21/- doz.º

106

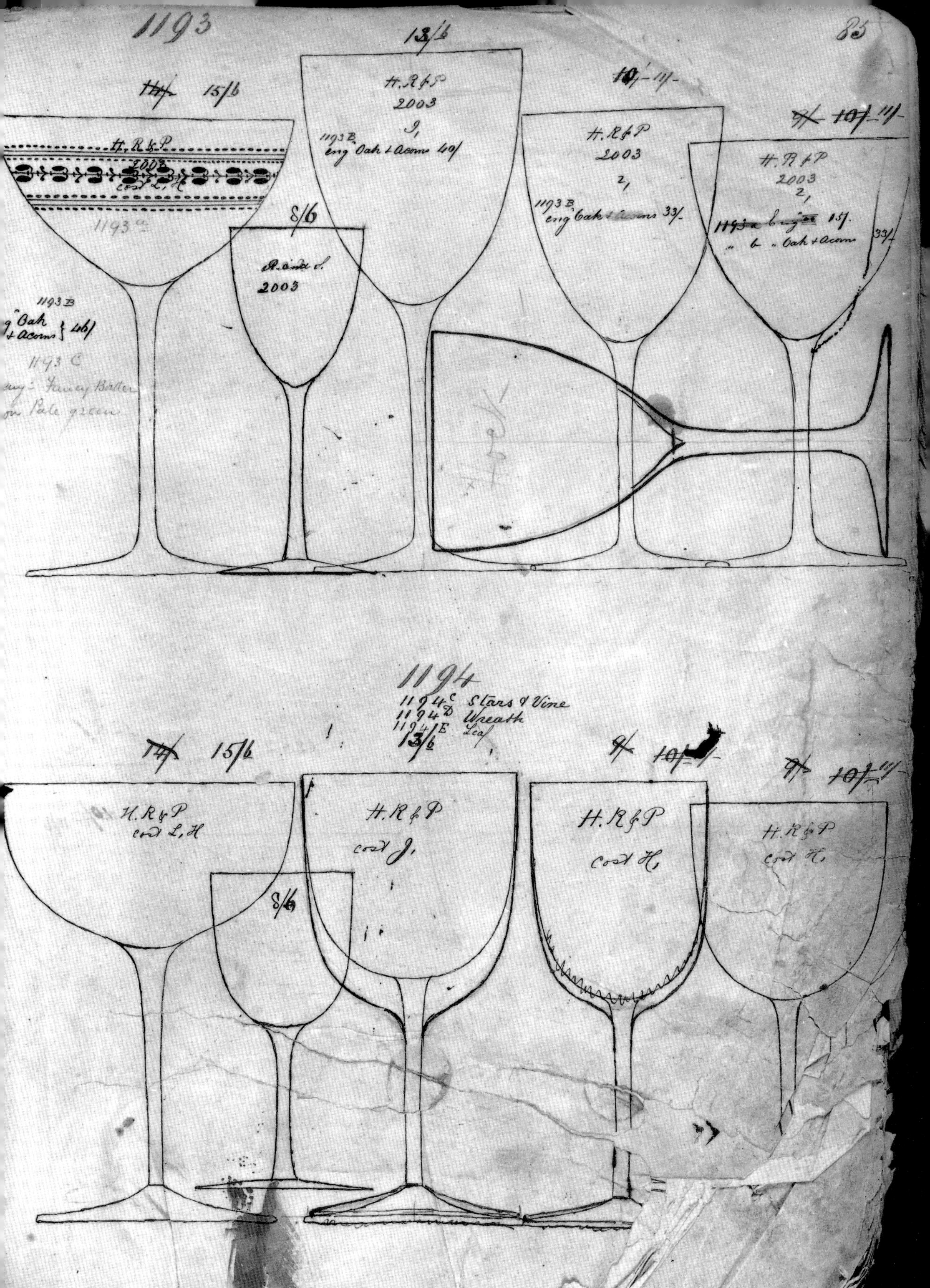

1193

13/6

14/ 15/6

10/- 14/-

9/- 10/- 14/-

tt. R & P
2003
cost L, H

1193 ª

1193 B
q Oah
+ Acorns } 46/

1193 C
eng: Fancy Border
on Pale green

8/6
R. C & C.
2003

1193 B
eng Oak & Acorns 40/

H. R & P
2003
9,

H. R & P
2003
2,

1193 B
eng. Oak & Acorns 33/

H. R & P
2003
2,

1193 eng 15/
" b " Oak + Acorns 33/

1194

1194 C   Stars & Vine
1194 D   Wreath
1194 E   Leaf

14/ 15/6

13/6

9/ 10/-

9/- 10/- 14/-

H. R & P
cost L, H

8/6

H. R & P
cost J,

H. R & P
cost H,

H. R & P
cost H,

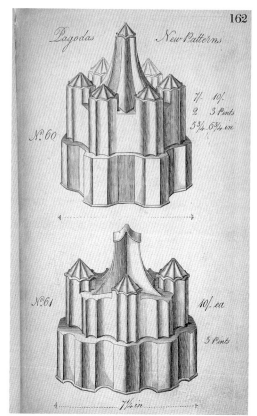

Pagodas — *New Patterns*

N.º 60 — 7/- 10/- — 2 3 Pints — 5¾ 6¾ in

N.º 61 — 10/- ea — 3 Pints — 7½ in

Pagodas. New Patterns.

N.º 62 — 5/- 5/6 6/- — 1½ 2 2½ Pint — 4¾ 5½ 6 in

N.º 63 — 8/- 9/- 10/- — 1½ 2 2½ Pint — 6 6½ 7 in — 7 in

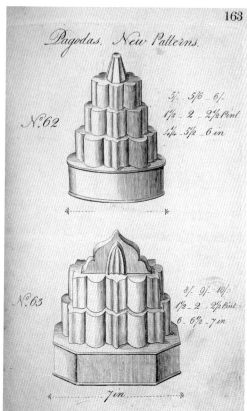

Pagodas — *New Patterns*

N.º 66 — 10/- — 7¼

67 — 12/- — 6¾

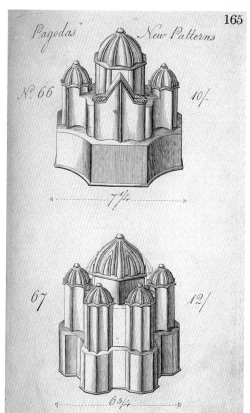

Pagodas — *New Patterns*

N.º 68 — 8/- — 7 in

N.º 69 — 9/- — 7 in

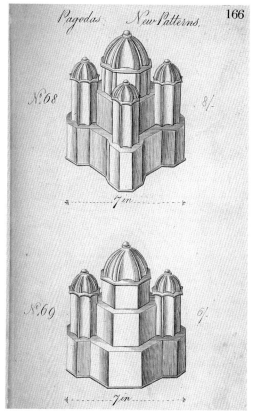

Pie Moulds. ass.d Patterns.

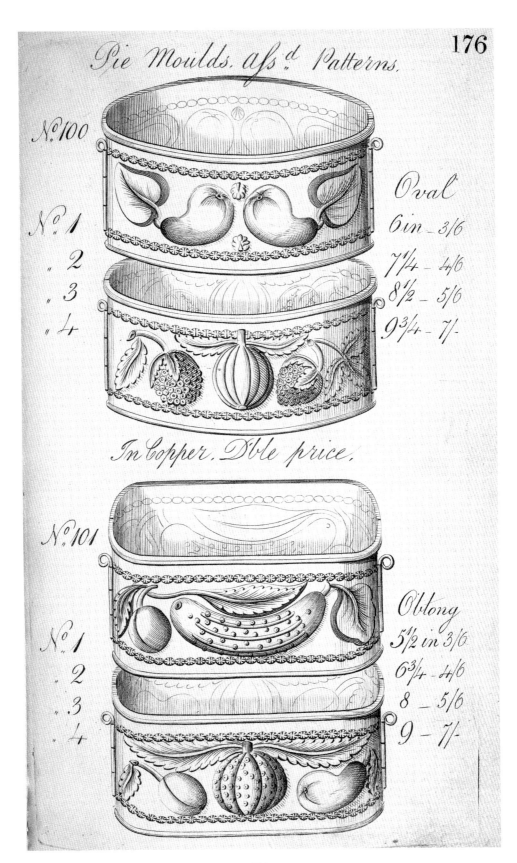

No.100

No.1
  " 2
  " 3
  " 4

Oval

6 in - 3/6
7¼ - 4/6
8½ - 5/6
9¾ - 7/-

In Copper. Dble price.

No.101

No.1
  " 2
  " 3
  " 4

Oblong

5½ in 3/6
6¾ - 4/6
8 - 5/6
9 - 7/-

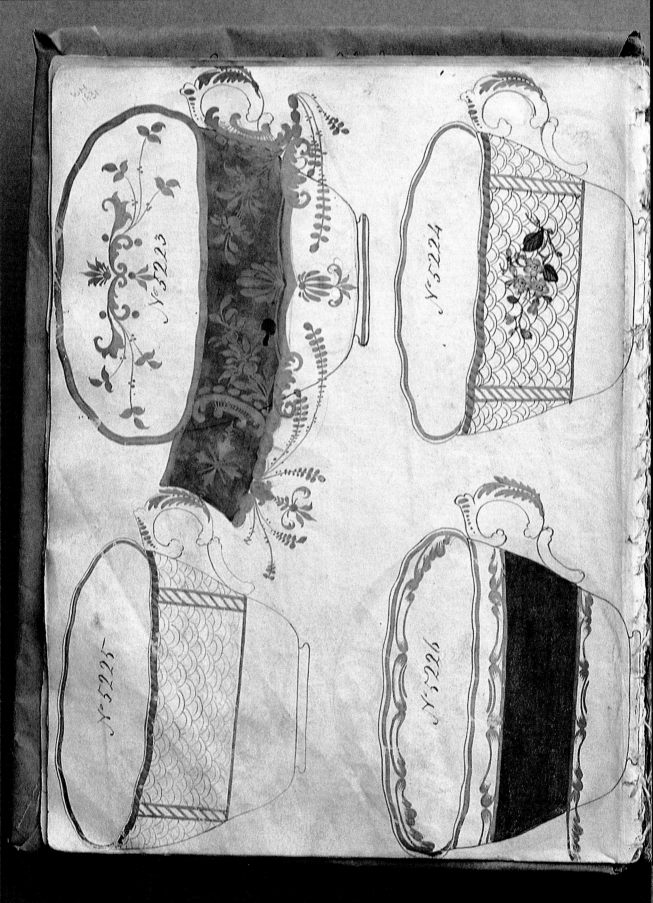

N° 5223

N° 5224

N° 5225

N° 5226

N° 5227

N° 5228

N° 5229

N° 5230

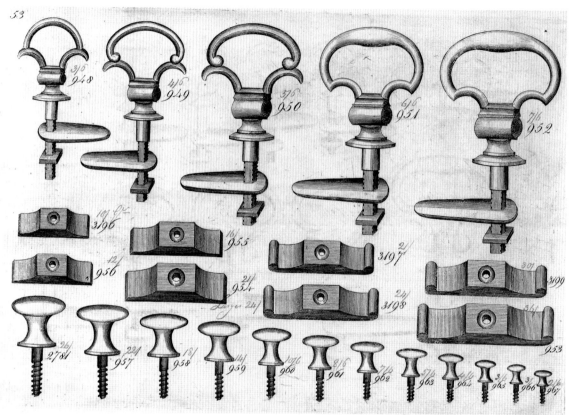

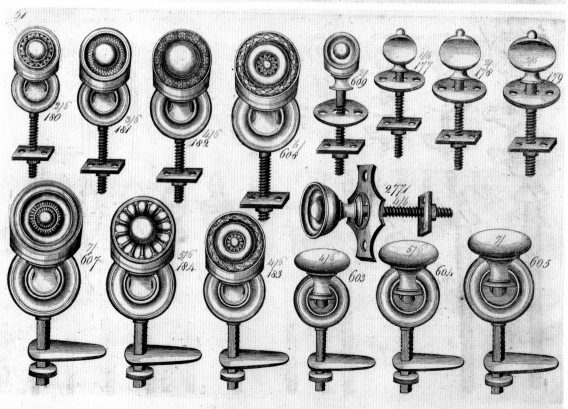

114

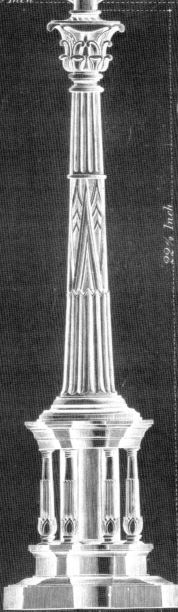

10 Inch

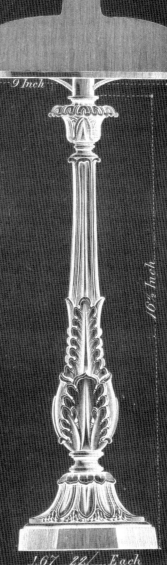

9 Inch

20 Inch

22½ Inch

16½ Inch

466 .... 2.6/ .... Each

429 .. 45/ .... Each

467 .. 22/ .. Each

DERBY CROWN PORCELAIN CO., LIMITED

by John Catis — Pinxton —

January 1840

Heart Leaf 1 Print Back 91 —

Walkers Cane 6 Print Back 19 —

Cows Convolvolus 7 Print Back 92 —

Sharps Rosette 6 prints Back 58 —

Talavera 3 print Back 61 —

Salamanca Edge — 3 print Back 92 —

Heart & Daisy — 8 prints 134 Back

Pannel Edge
4 Print Back

January 1841

Key Rosette   3 Prints Rack 331

Rose & Lily 7 Prints Rack 123

Walkers Rose Bud

Double Stock   7 Prints Rack 121
Centred 1874

Reed & Ribband

Fruit Border 3 Prints Rack 331

Anna Maria Garthwaite

Printed by Good & Son

Anna Maria Garthwaite. Nº 8 and 9.

Printed by Good & Son, 63, Bishopsgate Without.

255
255

256
256

257
257

J. G. CRACE. Dest. 1842.

4

High Victorian

AFTER *the Great* EXHIBITION

The decorative excesses of the Early Victorian period did abate somewhat in the years following the Great Exhibition of 1851. Even commercial furniture of the type manufactured by the firm of Gillow began to display cleaner, sharper lines, although the most important advances in design and the decorative arts were undoubtedly those made by the great innovators of the period: Morris, Burges, Talbert, Eastlake and Godwin. But apart from such 'art' designers, English factories continued to pour out an incredible array of products: textiles, furniture, ironwork, pottery, glass and many apparently ingenious gadgets.

Manufacturers' catalogues of the time are remarkable for the sheer volume of goods on offer: varieties of plated cutlery; different patterns of wrought-iron balconies; rounded and square, decorated and plain marble chimneypieces; and an amazing collection of devices, some of dubious worth and efficiency, such as the Portable Vapour Bath offered by Shoolbred, Loveridge & Shoolbred (illustrated on p. 155). This was indeed the great age of the gadget, of the application of new processes on a massive scale. Anything and everything, it seemed, could be manufactured.

Against this background of the proliferation of goods and artefacts, the reforming zeal of a small body of designers took on a new importance. Versions of the Gothic style still continued to be the main idiom of the reformers after the Great Exhibition. Pugin mounted his Medieval Court at the exhibition itself. In 1853 John Ruskin published his *Stones of Venice*, with its famous chapter on the nature of Gothic. The new Houses of Parliament by Barry and Pugin were completed in the 1860s in the Gothic style. But undoubtedly the dominant figure of the time was William Morris.

nlike the majority of his contemporaries, Morris did not accept machine manufacture as a necessary good. Realizing that the very organization of Victorian industrial society, in the workplace and in the home, militated against good design, Morris decided to go to the very roots of the design process by turning artist-craftsman, teaching himself various disciplines which gave him a real respect for the nature of materials and an understanding of the ways in which they could be worked. He was a designer of genius; his chintzes and wallpapers, although often based on historical or exotic models, have a fresh, incisive quality which set them quite apart from the fussy, confused historicism of pre-Exhibition and Exhibition designs. Tradition and originality are constantly combined in a beautifully balanced handling of the fundamentals of decoration and design. His furniture, too, has a fineness and simplicity which are in stark contrast to the befuddled elaboration of the eclectic mix which characterized the pieces of earlier decades. It wasn't that Morris eschewed historical models – far from it – but he always seemed to be able to select those elements, notably from traditional English country styles, which he could then combine in entirely convincing and contemporary designs.

he founding of William Morris's own firm in 1861 meant that the teachings of the master designer could be disseminated more effectively among like-minded spirits. Philip Webb and J.P. Seddon were directly associated with the Morris concern and both designed furniture which first appeared in the company catalogue for 1862. Much of the inspiration for their work was overtly medieval.

Painted furniture is surely one of the most distinctive and freshly innovative categories of design of the period. The most striking examples must be the secretaires and cabinets of William Burges (see pp. 152–153), whose virtuosity in combining monumental forms and painted planes in a roughly Gothic format sets him apart as one of the truly adventurous designers of the latter half of the nineteenth century. Other influential reforming figures – largely through the wide dissemination of their designs – include Bruce Talbert, whose *Gothic Forms Applied to Furniture* appeared in 1867-68, and Charles Lock Eastlake. The latter's *Hints on Household Taste* of 1868 was reprinted many times and had a profound influence on design, mainly because the author focused his attention on the domestic interior, producing simple but stylish designs for whole room settings and sturdy, uncomplicated furniture.

Other design influences joined the reform movement, notably the taste for *japonisme*, the cult of things Japanese,

with special attention to the swirling lines of the Japanese print-makers. Their work had been included in the London 1862 Exhibition and was already being collected by leading aesthetes, notably by E.W. Godwin, who later became a design consultant to the firm of Liberty. He was also a friend of the painter Whistler for whom he designed the White House in Tite Street, Chelsea, in 1878. Godwin's design ethos introduced a lighter touch in the midst of the sturdy Gothic of other reformers. His furniture is distinctly Anglo-Japanese, often in ebonised wood, and once again publication ensured the dissemination of the style – in William Watt's *Art Furniture* catalogue of 1877, and in *Decoration and Furniture of Town Houses* of 1881 by Robert Edis. Godwin's extensive sketch-books are now held in the Department of Prints and Drawings of the Victoria & Albert Museum, London.

t would be misleading, though, to see the whole of English design of the post-Exhibition years as being informed by reforming zeal. Historicism was still a powerful force, notably in interior decoration and complete room settings, which therefore affected the design of individual elements, notably furniture, textiles and wallpaper. In architecture, too, a new nostalgia for a classical past began to emerge, typified by the so-called Queen Anne Revival associated with the architects Norman Shaw and Eden Nesfield. 'Renaissance' styles began to be more in evidence from 1870 onwards; significantly, Walter Pater published his *Studies in the History of the Renaissance* in 1873. This new classicism, though, is characterized by a heavy, ponderous quality, far removed from the delicacy and lightness of eighteenth-century Neoclassicism. One design element typical of the period was the massive, almost architectural, overmantel, complete with pediment and niches for the display of decorative objects.

uch revivalism was to continue well into the Edwardian era. But, from the Great Exhibition onwards, the debate as to what constitutes good design had been fully engaged, in the swatch books, catalogues and pattern books of the era. It was a debate that was shortly to lead to one of the most magnificent flowerings of English design – the Arts and Crafts Movement.

page 128 This fragment of wallpaper, printed from wooden blocks in the third quarter of the nineteenth century, was recovered from Lanhydrock House, Cornwall.

opposite An early Victorian power-loom for weaving tufted pile carpets.

4
AFTER
the Great
EXHIBITION

A 'modern dining room' from a drawing of 1872 by H.W. Batley; Batley later published a *Series of Studies for Furniture, Decoration etc.* in 1883.

The first stirrings of the reforming spirit in English design which culminated in the finest achievements of the Arts and Crafts Movement began to show themselves during the third quarter of the nineteenth century. William Morris began business in the 1860s, while William De Morgan (1839-1917), undoubtedly the Movement's greatest potter, began to produce pottery and tiles to designs such as these in London in 1869, later moving to Morris's Merton Abbey in 1882.

Whether in mainstream furniture production, ecclesiastical furnishings, or as a vocabulary for the great designers of the age, versions of the Gothic style played a dominant role in the design history of mid to late nineteenth-century England.

Pugin and Ruskin urged its claims to pre-eminence after the Great Exhibition of 1851, and the greatest building project of the age – the new Houses of Parliament – turned out to be a Gothic masterpiece. These two designs for Gothic-style chairs are by Turner & Sons; they are reproduced from a folder of etchings of hundreds of variations by anonymous craftsmen and designers now held in the Victoria & Albert Museum, London. A simpler form of Gothic eventually became the style of design reform.

Although there was undoubtedly much increased attention to the need for good design after the recognized failures of the Great Exhibition, historicism and eclecticism nevertheless remained powerful forces for decades to come. Albums of complete room settings, such as these published by T. Knight & Sons in varieties of historical styles, were a staple of the interior decorating business. And the demand for such settings clearly affected the design of individual elements, especially furniture, textiles and wallpaper.

Catalogues of virtually every type of household product abounded in late Victorian England, a reflection of the country's increasing economic might and the accompanying growth of the domestic market. Compared to the standardization which has characterized much of twentieth-century domestic design, the individuality of the variety of beds offered on this page is striking. Many of them hint at the Gothic in their pavilion-like forms, suggesting the medieval themes so beloved by Morris and his followers.

Ironwork in the form of railings and balconies decorated the façades of even the humblest terraced house in Victorian London. Catalogues offered standard designs to the builders of the massed houses of the inner city. Grander projects, however, such as this design for the Green Park façade of no. 20 Arlington Street, would attract an individual touch. This design, by L.W. Collmann, is executed in pen and ink, pencil and watercolour.

Like Morris and De Morgan, Christopher Dresser (1834-1904) was active as a designer throughout the latter part of the nineteenth century, from the 1860s until the full flowering of the Arts and Crafts Movement. He designed for a wide variety of media, including pottery, textiles, wallpapers, furniture, metalwork and glass. An enthusiastic botanist, his early designs (those reproduced here date from 1861) show a preoccupation with adapting and transforming natural forms to decorative ornament. Always active in promoting good design, Dresser was later editor of *The Furniture Gazette.*

The productions of Shoolbred, Loveridge & Shoolbred (see p. 155) typified the High Victorian fascination with the gadget. New ideas – some sound, some unsound – were applied in profusion to the production of household wares, and nowhere more so than to those for the bathroom. Presumably the shower-head of the Oval Pillar Bath (p. 147) could be raised or lowered by the winding mechanism.

4
AFTER
the Great
EXHIBITION

In common with a number of English and Continental potteries, in the 1850s and 1860s Wedgwood introduced a number of designs derived from the Italian painted *maiolica* of the sixteenth century. 'Majolica', as it was termed, was shown extensively by Minton's at the Great Exhibition and in the following decades coloured glaze coupled with relief decoration was applied to all manner of domestic objects, including umbrella stands and *jardinières*. Wedgwood's reaction to this market opportunity was to revive production of their eighteenth-century green-glaze ware, with decorations of botanical forms. These designs are taken from one of three 'majolica' pattern books in the Wedgwood archive: 'Apple Blossom flower pot' (p. 148) and 'Shell Oyster tray' (p. 149) (see p. 203).

Best known as a painter, Sir Edward Burne-Jones (1833-98) also had a close association with William Morris as a designer, notably of tapestries and stained-glass windows. This sketch, inspired by

Chaucer's *The Legend of Good Women*, is a preliminary study for embroidered wall-hangings which were to have graced the house of John Ruskin. The project was never completed, although the needlework may have been begun. The figures represented include Cleopatra, Dido, Medea, Ariadne and Philomene, all martyrs to love; the names of the proposed seamstresses were written above the figure on which it was intended they should eventually work.

The furniture which William Burges (1827-81) designed in his entirely distinctive manner was either intended for his own house or for the major decorative schemes he undertook for the Marquess of Bute at Cardiff Castle and Castle Coch. Gothic in overall style, the forms of his furniture are relatively simple, as these designs for a cupboard and secretaire, but the brilliant surface decoration places it among the most innovative achievements of nineteenth-century design. The painting drew on a variety of figurative subjects, including birds and flowers and scenes from the Bible and pagan mythology.

Artists commissioned by Burges included Burne-Jones, H. Stacy Marks, Albert Moore, E.J. Poynter and Simeon Solomon.

Providing as much choice as possible for the customer – probably a jobbing builder – was clearly an underlying principle of the activities of Henry Greene & Co., manufacturers of fireplace surrounds in a variety of materials. This page is reproduced from one of their trade catalogues of *c*. 1880-90, part of the archive now held in the Geffrye Museum, London.

Another example of ingenious Victorian gadgetry: the Portable Vapour Bath was offered in two models by Shoolbred, Loveridge & Shoolbred at 30 shillings. It purported to allow sufferers of rheumatism to undergo beneficial treatment in the home, presumably clad in dressing-gown and slippers. Based in Wolverhampton, the company epitomized the spirit of late Victorian manufacture in the ambitious range of its trade catalogues, which also offered

slipper and shower baths and basins, coffee pots and urns, seamless cooking vessels, tea and coffee pots.

The fresh, incisive wallpaper designs of the William Morris firm – revolutionary when compared with the fussy historicism of Great Exhibition design – were among the first successful examples of the reforming spirit in design which began to show itself in England during the 1860s. Traditional subject-matter is rendered new and exciting by the boldness of the design. These samples, part of the record of the Morris firm's output maintained by Jeffrey & Co., are pasted into an old account book, accompanied by code numbers, pattern names and other annotations. Each published colouring of every pattern was recorded, since new ones were added after the original publication of the design. These records are now in the archive of Arthur Sanderson & Sons Ltd.

The firm of Elkington & Co. Ltd., now a subsidiary of the

4

AFTER
the Great
EXHIBITION

Delta Metal Co. Ltd., had its origins in the early part of the nineteenth century, when George Richard Elkington (1801-65) and his cousin Henry Elkington (*c.* 1812-52) patented their methods of gilding base metal in 1836 and 1837. By 1840 they had perfected their technique of electroplating, and the company's first factories were established in London, Birmingham, Liverpool and Dublin, with a showroom in London. The company records for the nineteenth century and for the first part of the twentieth (now held in the Victoria & Albert Museum, London) contain a large number of original drawings, with annotation. These pages of ornate candelabra designs are taken from the record book for 1840-73, one of 26 similar volumes in the archive.

pages 160–161

One fascinating aspect of Morris's preserved designs is the sense they give of the designer's activity still continuing. The archive pattern 'Daisy' (p. 160), printed as a wallpaper in 1864, bears traces of layers of pencil lines, as the artist changed the position of the leaves and then used wash to conceal the

changes. Only the birds appear to be in final form, unlike those in the 'Bird' pattern (p. 161) which seem to be independent of the background.

pages 162–163

Philip Webb (1831-1915) was yet another relatively long-lived designer who worked successfully during the final decades of the Victorian era and into the full flowering of Arts and Crafts at the turn of the century. He was closely associated with Morris, for whom he designed the Red House at Bexleyheath in 1860, where he seemed deliberately to eschew classical features in favour of an English rustic vernacular with some dashing touches of modernism. From 1861 Webb worked exclusively with Morris, designing furniture, metalwork and glass, until 1875 when he resigned his partnership in the firm. These elegant designs for champagne glasses were manufactured by the Whitefriars glass factory and may have been created as early as 1859.

pages 164–165

The design of flat patterns, for whatever medium, was

dominated in this period by William Morris. His equivalent in ceramics, specifically earthenware, was William De Morgan (see p. 137). After a period at Merton Abbey he set up a factory in Fulham in 1888, where his output was characterized by patterns derived from Persian, Greek and fifteenth-century southern Spanish wares. His decorative plates in lustre painted earthenware display stylized yet vibrant designs in colours which De Morgan referred to as 'Persian' – green, black and turquoise.

pages 166–167

This double-page of designs for butter knives is taken from the exhaustive production records of Elkington & Co. Ltd. The designs are meticulously hand-drawn in black ink on cartridge paper; the pages of the pattern books are indexed. This, the first of the 26, also contains designs for butter boats, butter coolers, candelabra, claret jugs, cups and tankards. In the same archive are 10 volumes of company history, administrative papers, press cuttings, company deeds, account books and general correspondence.

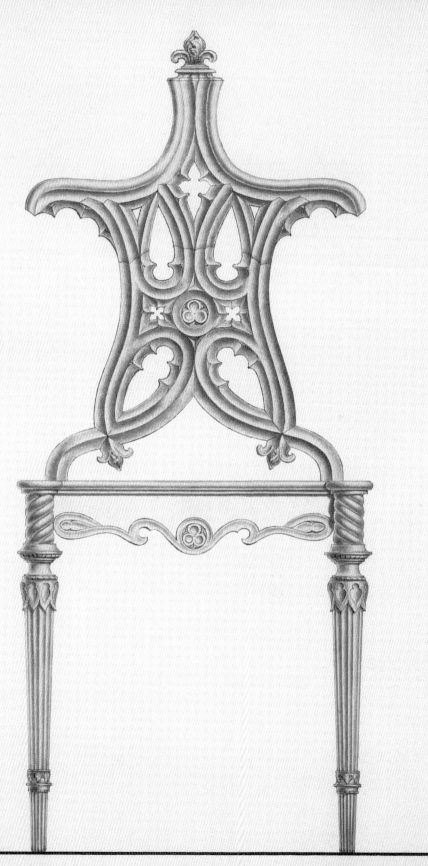

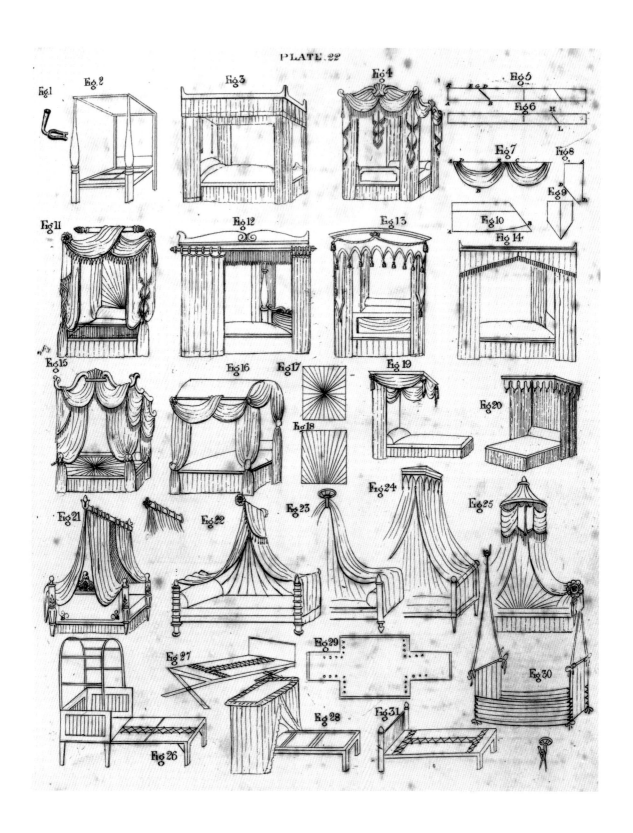

PLATE. 22

Fig. 1 Fig. 2 Fig. 3 Fig. 4 Fig. 5 Fig. 6 Fig. 7 Fig. 8 Fig. 9 Fig. 10 Fig. 11 Fig. 12 Fig. 13 Fig. 14 Fig. 15 Fig. 16 Fig. 17 Fig. 18 Fig. 19 Fig. 20 Fig. 21 Fig. 22 Fig. 23 Fig. 24 Fig. 25 Fig. 26 Fig. 27 Fig. 28 Fig. 29 Fig. 30 Fig. 31

20 ARLINGTON STREET.
IRON WORK TO PARK FRONT.
Scale ½ in = 1ft.

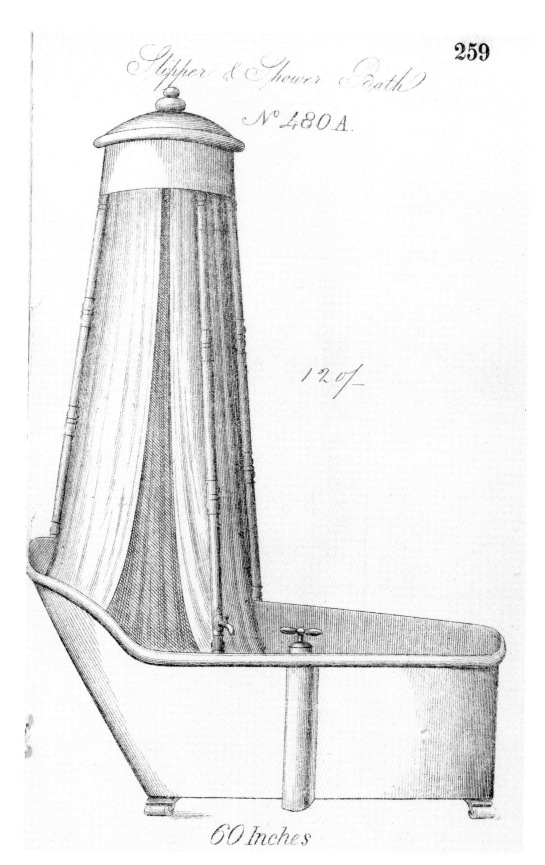

Slipper & Shower Bath

Nº 480 A.

12/-

60 Inches

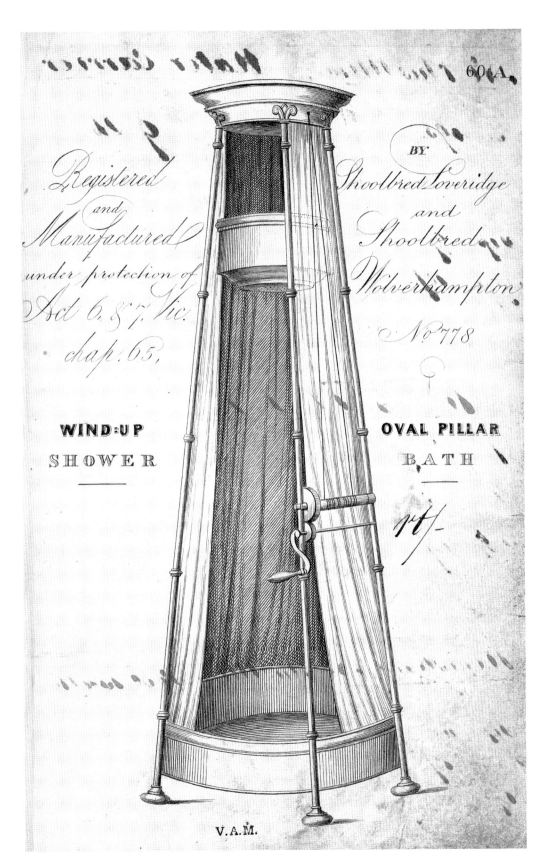

60A.

Registered
and
Manufactured
under protection of
Act 6 & 7 Vic.
chap. 65,

BY

Shoolbred Loveridge
and
Shoolbred
Wolverhampton
No 778

WIND-UP

SHOWER

OVAL PILLAR

BATH

14/-

V.A.M.

148

No 2947   Shell Oyster Tray   See Pattern

White

Olive green

Crimson

Shaded in
Crimson & Lavender

Shaded in M Brown
Crimson

Pale
in Yellow

New
green

Celery

White
Ivory

White

Crimson

Shaded in Pink
Lavender
ground

M Brown

Olive

No 2948   Shell Oyster Tray   See Pattern

White Foam

Dutch green

Mottled
in
Pink Brown
Yellow Brown
& Grey

Yellow
green

Shaded in
V.g. Yellow

Ivory

Grey

White

Crimson

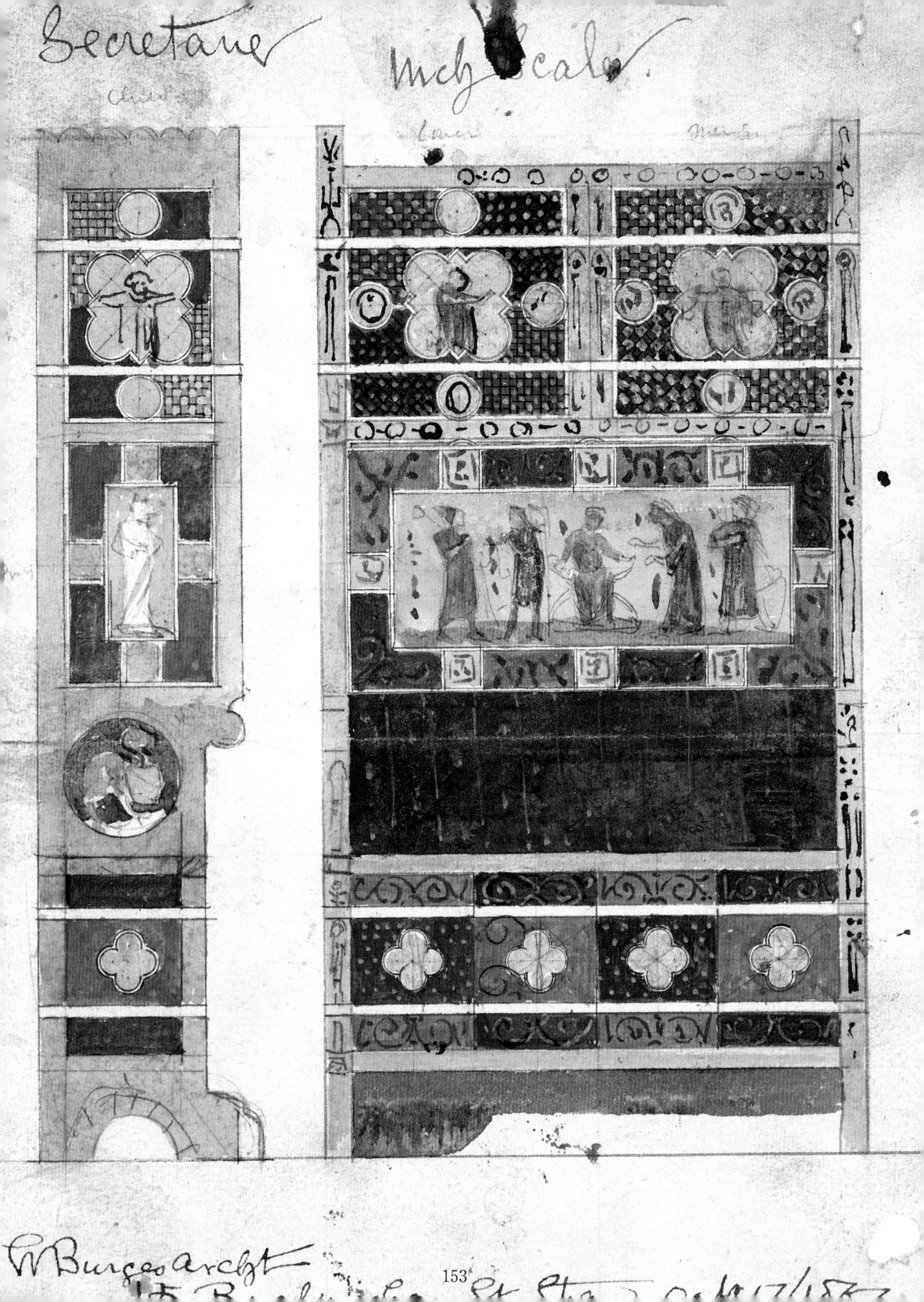
Secretaire
W Burges archt

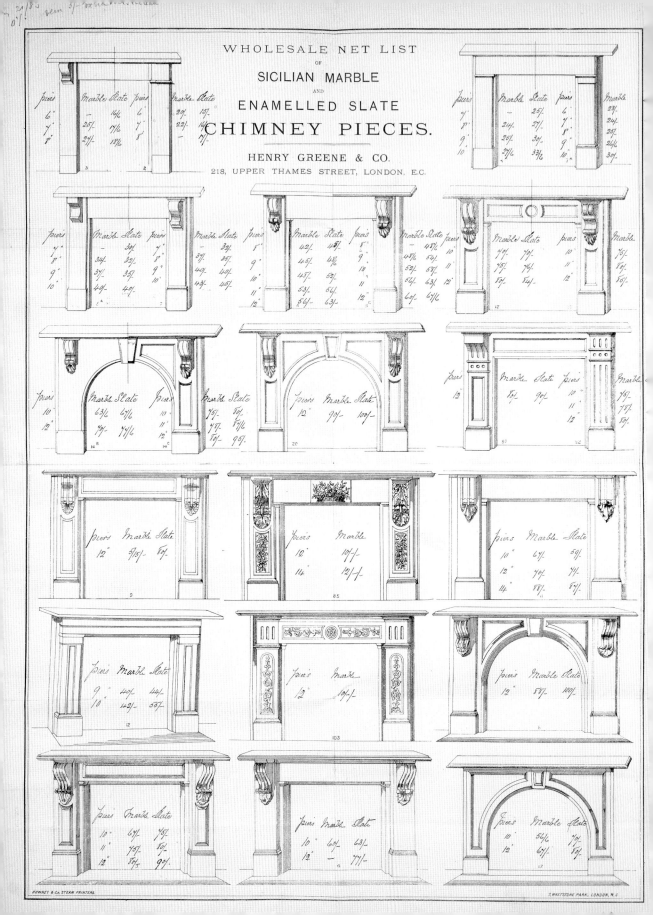

WHOLESALE NET LIST
OF
SICILIAN MARBLE
AND
ENAMELLED SLATE
CHIMNEY PIECES.

HENRY GREENE & CO.
218, UPPER THAMES STREET, LONDON, E.C.

Nº 691

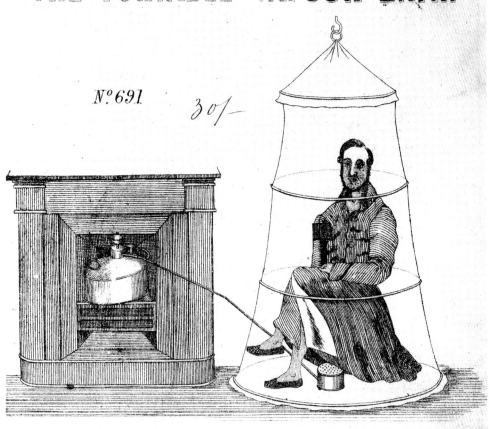

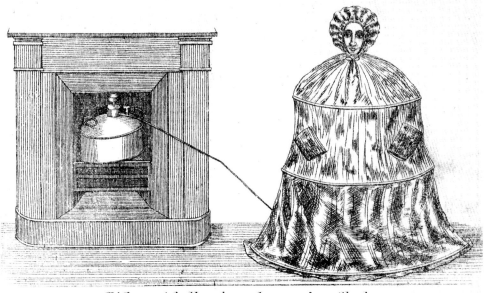

Either with Hood, or Suspension Cloth.

Safe

all Safe

1 Bur ... ether Safe

Safe

7 Blocks Lilly Dado 15 x 26 . 0098		
1 extra for 2nd Backsm }	12	0
Rack 133		
6 Blocks Margarete 21 x 15 002294	8	9
Rack 128		
2 extra Blocks 002667 Alcesta Frye	3	3
Barratt 24-24" Blocks 002295	36	0
Rack 114		
One Frieze 8 Block	11	10
Barratt 100192		
One Tower 3 Blocks	4	10
Paper 2¾ sheets do	5	18
Frieze 6 Blocks	6	
Dado 3 - 75¼º	5	
Barratt Ivy 6 Black 21.	12	
Black 114		
Barratt 00125 Rack 89		
Tulip 2ᵈ print Safe		
Barratt Azalea 001107 12. 21.	20	-
Rack 109		

£.6
Barratt

Barratt

Chain patt
(4 cols) Safe

Safe

Safe
Safe

Kirk Border

Boat
freize

Sevan dado

all Parts Safe

Beauthy 1Block Barratt	002234	
3 – 15"	6.	0
61874 Destroyd	Rack	
Dwarf		
Barratt ?		
4e Colr		
62012	7	10
Rus. Feb.	Rack	
00316		
Barratt		
61592		
3 – 12"	5	
Gowan	Rack 138	

62050 Crane's Iris 001207 Rack. 11. Blocks Rack. 135 — 17
6215 Rushes 140 2. 002613 140 — 4. 10.
140 3. 140 126 — 3 5
Ceiling Sign 62140.
" Border 60402 02655

Rack 132-133
Kirk Domed 0378 Blocks — Barratt Fin 57 0
153 001104 8 4" Blocks 6. 12" do Rack 157 Sevan Dado 21. 0
51 002444 001269
51 0R 007288 60200 8 3/4. Blocks Boat 17 10
153 Sevan dado Safe
Rack 157/158

Elder see back

Plum 61415 Barratt Rack 143
Marigold Border 60354 Plum — 18
5 Blocks Laurel
002269
1Bine freize 60351 Marigold — 6 10
5 Blocks
002373 Bine 6
Laurel Dado 61390
5 Blocks

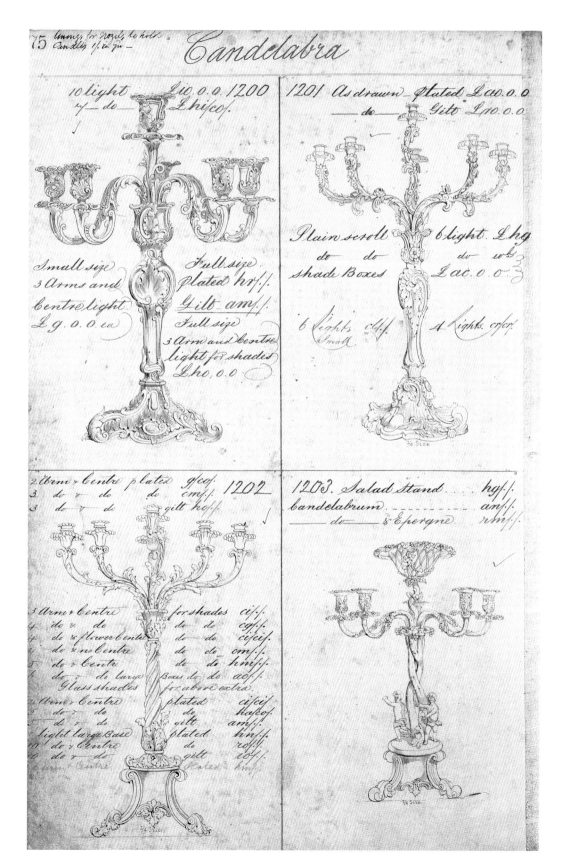

Candelabra

75 Arms for Nozels, to hold
Candles 1/. ea gм —

10 light ___ £10.0.0 1200
7 — do ___ £ his cos.

1201 As drawn Fluted £10.0.0
___ do ___ Gilt £10.0.0

Plain scroll ___ 6 light. £ hg
do ___ do ___ do ___ wh
shade Boxes ___ £ ac.0.0

6 lights cs/.
Small
4 lights. cr/cs.

Small size
3 Arms and
Centre light
£ 9.0.0 ea

Full size
Plated hr/.
Gilt am/.

Full size
3 Arm and Centre
light for shades
£ho.0.0

¾ Size

2 Arm & Centre plated g/cos.
3 do & do do cm/.
3 do & do gilt ho/.

1202

1203. Salad Stand ___ hg/.
Candelabrum ___ an/.
___ do ___ & Epergne ___ rm/.

5 Arm & Centre ___ for shades c/.
4 do & do do do cq/.
4 do & flower Centre do do c/c/.
4 do & no Centre do do cm/.
5 do & Centre do do hm/.
5 do & do large Boxes do do ao/.
Glass shades for above extra
5 Arm & Centre plated c/c/.
5 do & do do ha/cos.
5 do & do gilt am/.
7 light large Base plated hm/.
10 do & Centre do ro/.
10 do & do gilt io/.

¾ Size

⅔ Size

2466   Candelabrum & Epergne — rn/./
       do —— & —— do — gilt — ig/./

Candelabrum
& Epergne w.
saucers for
Epergne.
mi/./
Cand.rn only — ag/./

10 light
Cand.rn
only — rm/./
w.t Basket.
mm/./
Salad stand only — tq/./

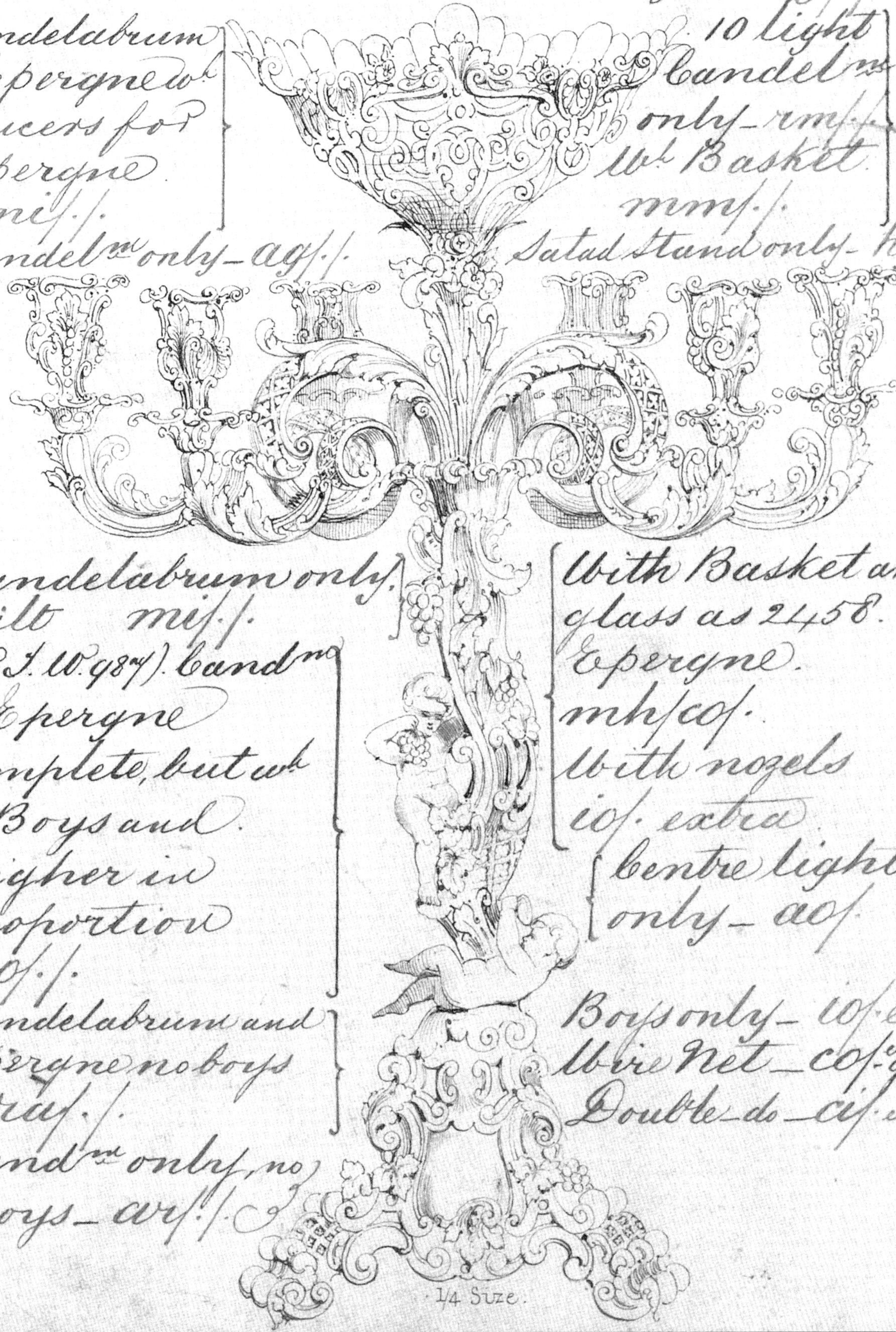

Candelabrum only,
gilt   mi/./
(or S.W.987) Cand.rn
& Epergne
complete, but w.t
3 Boys and.
higher in
proportion
co/./

With Basket and
glass as 2458.
Epergne.
mh/co/.
With nozels
io/. extra
Centre light
only — ao/

Candelabrum and
Epergne no boys
ru/./
Cand.rn only, no
Boys — ar/./

Boys only — co/. ea
Wire Net — co/. grass
Double do — ci/. in do

1/4 Size.

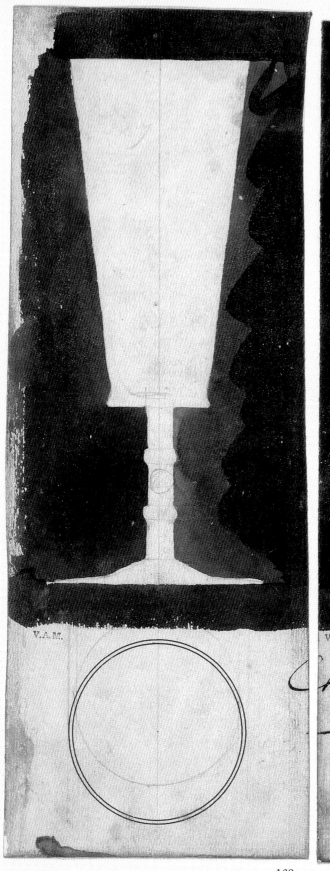

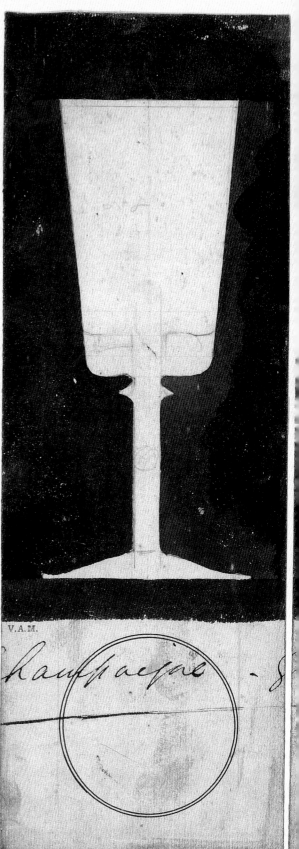

V.A.M.

V.A.M.

Chauffacque

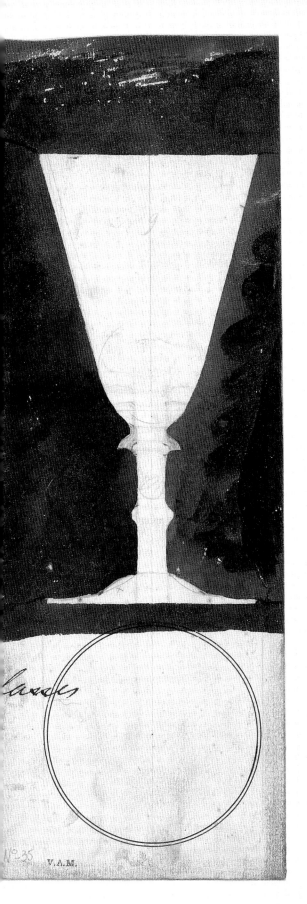

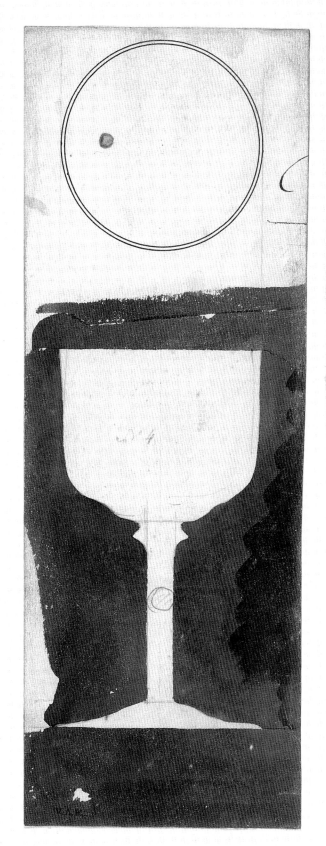

Butter Knives

4380

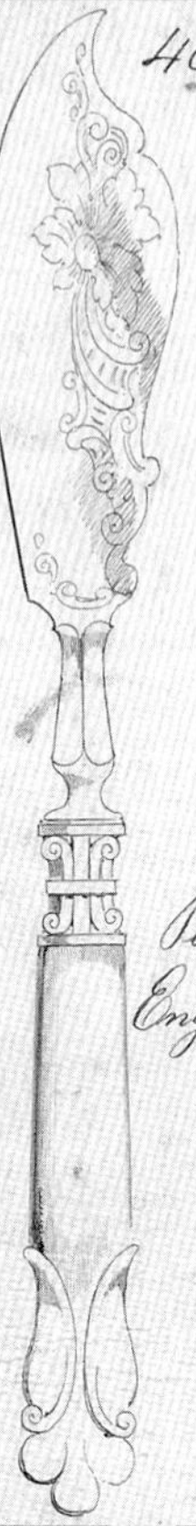

4381

4382

4420

Error.

See Pickle Forks

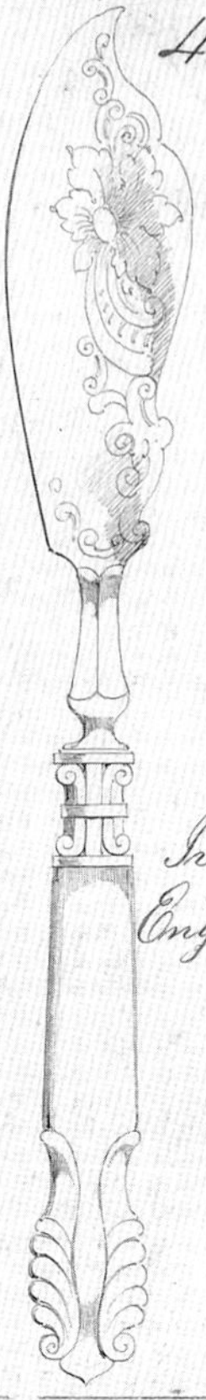

Pearl.
Eng'd cop.

Ivory
Eng'd cop.

Full Size.

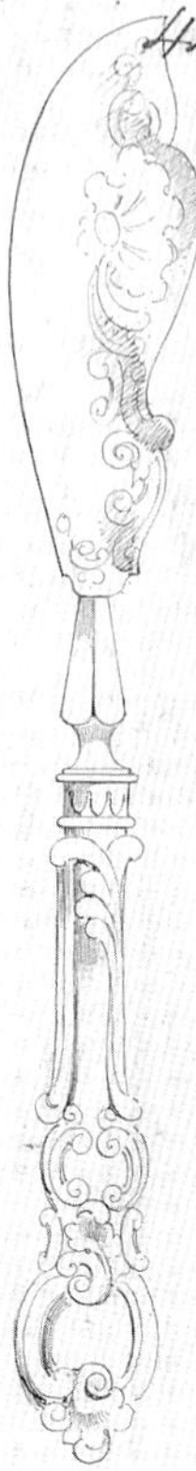

Full Size.

9/i

Full Size.

4421

4422

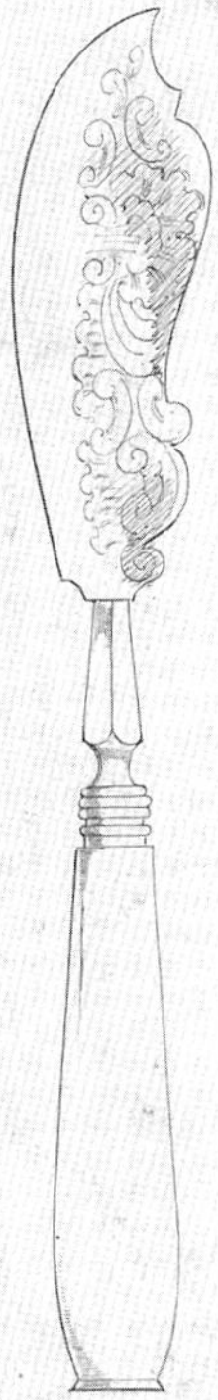

4423

4424

Ivory n/p

Pearl cop.

Eng'd Pearl. plain 9/i
9/i Ivory
9/i Ivory

Butter Knives.

4425.	4426.	4427	4428

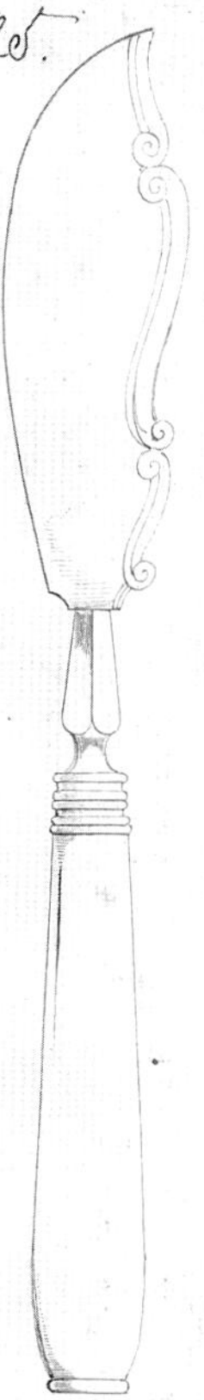

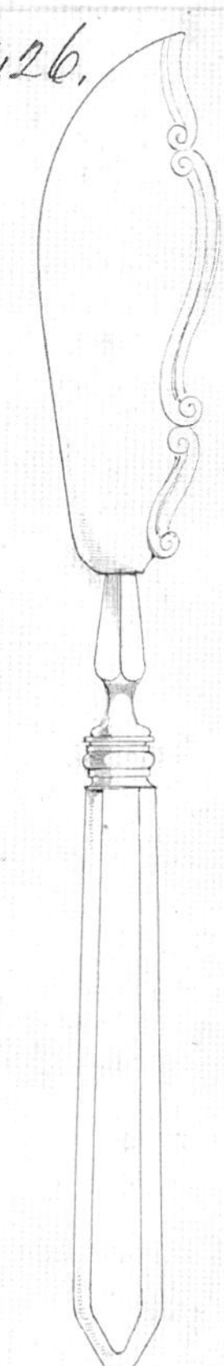

Plain 7/6
Engd 9/–

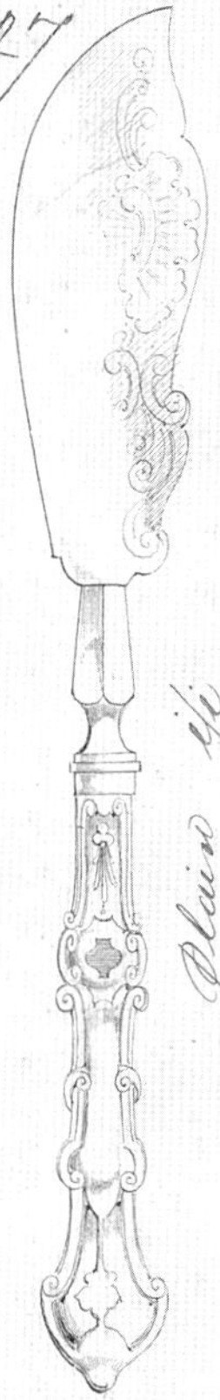

Plain 7/
Engd 9/6

Full Size | Full Size | Full Size | Full Size

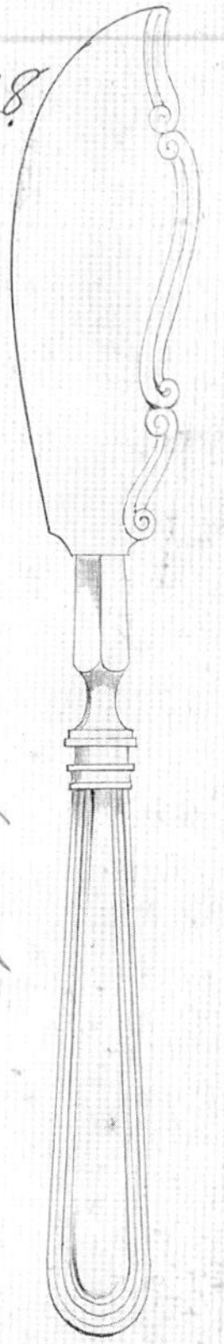

4429	4430	4431	4432

Ivory Engd 9/–

Ivory Engd 9/–

Lily handle chasd Blade 11/

Full Size | Full Size | Full Size | Full Size

5

The Late 19th Century

INTO

RTS *and*

CRAFTS

The emergence of a distinctly new, yet emphatically
English aesthetic in the latter part of the nineteenth
century is one of the most fascinating chapters in the
history of design. However, the chronology of the Arts
and Crafts Movement, as the new design came to be
known, is not straightforward; generations of firms
and individuals overlapped from the eighteen-seventies
onwards. Even as late as 1890 William Morris had still
to establish his last great enterprise, the Kelmscott Press
(a major factor in elevating the status of English printing
and typographical design throughout the western
world). But there were a number of unifying aspects
in the works and writings of most of the leading
practitioners of the style: a belief in the dignity of the
craftsman as an essential concomitant to good design,
and an acknowledgment of the seminal influence of
William Morris and John Ruskin.

Central to the teachings of Ruskin was the demolition
of the distinction between the fine and applied arts;
from now on, the design of interiors and related artefacts
was to be as important as the creation of painting
and sculpture – just as the decoration of ecclesiastical
buildings had been at the time of the Renaissance. At a
lecture in Bradford in 1859, he adduced Correggio's work
in Parma churches and Tintoretto's decoration of the

Great School of San Rocco in Venice as examples of the successful combination of the fine and decorative arts. He was also concerned that the latter and, especially, architecture should reflect the permanent underlying forms of nature, although this part of Ruskin's teaching was often much more literally interpreted by *fin-de-siècle* designers on the Continent than by their English counterparts. Nevertheless, integrity and congruity of materials and form were major concerns of the English designer-craftsmen of the period.

n the last two decades of the nineteenth century a number of guilds and societies were established which reflected the new respectability of the applied arts and the pre-eminence of the artist-craftsman. There is more than a note of medievalist nostalgia in some of their names: A.H. Mackmurdo's Century Guild of 1882, the Art Workers' Guild of 1884, C.R. Ashbee's Guild of Handicraft of 1888, the Arts and Crafts Exhibition Society of the same year, and the Birmingham Guild of Handicraft of 1900.

Many of the designers affiliated to these guilds were of a generation younger than Morris (1834-96), but two of the most interesting (whose original work is represented in the illustration pages which follow) were virtual contemporaries: William De Morgan (1839-1917) and Christopher Dresser (1834-1904).

De Morgan was undoubtedly the great English potter of the late nineteenth century and, as a designer, close to Morris. He began production in London in the early eighteen-seventies, turning out decorated pots and tiles in earthenware. His role, though, was very much that of artist-designer rather than craftsman-potter, since he generally left the actual application of his largely blue and green palette to others. His sketches and watercolours show a lively appreciation of the relationship between form and pattern, often in a 'Persian' style, another instance of the late-century fascination with exotic design.

hristopher Dresser was, effectively, one of the first professional designers for industrial production. He taught design at South Kensington and published a number of significant books on the relationship of design and ornament. He travelled extensively in Japan and the Far East during 1877 and returned with a large collection of Oriental works of art; his book *Japan* was published in 1882. Like De Morgan, Dresser designed pottery, mainly decorative earthenware for the Linthorpe Pottery near Middlesbrough. He was also an ardent botanist, and his work certainly shows a preoccupation with adapting natural forms to decorative ornament. His Clutha glass vases, designed for James Couper of Glasgow, are richly curvilinear, almost organic in shape. In his *Principles of Decorative Design* (1873), Dresser wrote: 'I have sought to embody the one idea of power, energy, force, or vigour...

I have employed such lines as we see in the bursting buds of spring, when the energy of growth is at its maximum....'.

English furniture design of the period, especially in interiors conceived as coordinated schemes of related artefacts, produced work of great craftsmanship and elegance. The names of the men who turned their hands to it form a catalogue of the highest achievement in European terms: A.H. Mackmurdo, C.F.A. Voysey, C.R. Ashbee, W.R. Lethaby, W.H. Baillie Scott, whose most stylish furniture was made for the New Palace at Darmstadt, without forgetting the innovations taking place to the north in the revolutionary designs of C.R. Mackintosh and the Glasgow School.

et, the English craft tradition, as it was interpreted by the Arts and Crafts Movement, was perhaps best expressed by the designers and cabinet-makers who came to be known collectively as the Cotswold School. Kenton & Co. had originally been established in 1890 by a group of architects, including Ernest Gimson, W.R. Lethaby and Sidney Barnsley. In 1891 the group held a first exhibition at Barnard's Inn, Holborn, but in 1893 Gimson and Barnsley started to look outside London for a suitable place to establish a workshop, finally settling in specially built premises at Sapperton.

The designs of the group drew heavily on English country furniture traditions: ladder-back chairs, capacious cupboards and refectory tables. Both Gimson and Barnsley had immense respect for the materials they used, and most pieces show fine workmanship in the use of the wood. Much of the work was carried out by local craftsmen; any metal parts, such as handles, were made by the local blacksmith. In this linking of designer and workman, the work of the Cotswold School was one of the purest expressions of Arts and Crafts ideals.

One relatively unsung hero of this particularly fecund period of English design is Archibald Knox, Liberty's most prolific designer of metalware. Knox had come to London from his native Isle of Man in the 1890s when, it has been suggested, he worked in the design studio of Christopher Dresser. The drawings reproduced on pp. 170 and 190–191 show a consummate mastery of the intricate tracery of traditional Celtic ornament, combined with a pure sense of overall line and form. In the bold originality of his handling of technical problems and in his appreciation of the importance of elegant designs which properly serve a purpose, Knox could stand as one of the purest practitioners of the Arts and Crafts ideal.

page 168 An undated pencil design by Ernest Gimson for a plasterwork frieze.

opposite The workshop of the Charles Knowles & Co. factory, London *c.* 1904; established in 1852, the firm produced high-quality block-printed wallpapers.

5

INTO ARTS
and
CRAFTS

A drawing by T. Raffles Davison, executed in 1890, of the drawing room at Bullers Wood, Chislehurst; the interior decoration had been completed by Morris & Co. in 1889.

Perhaps more than any other group of designers, the furniture-makers of the Cotswold School – Ernest Gimson and Sidney Barnsley – were responsible for reinterpreting the English vernacular craft tradition in the context of the Arts and Crafts Movement. After beginnings in London as Kenton & Co., the group finally settled in the Cotswolds, where their designs strongly reflected English country furniture traditions, concentrating on solid, well-made pieces like ladder-back chairs, cupboards, chests-of-drawers, and refectory tables. Most of the drawings of the group, from the establishment of Kenton & Co. until the deaths of the principal designers, are now held by Cheltenham Art Gallery and Museums. These undated sketches for two writing cabinets are by Ernest Gimson.

Metalwork became one of the major areas of English design achievement in the latter part of the nineteenth century, notably in the hands of C.R. Ashbee and his Guild of Handicraft. Another successful figure in helping to spread appreciation of design for metalwork and enamelling was Alexander Fisher who began to teach from his studio in 1887 and later became head of the enamelling department at the Central School of Arts and Crafts in 1896. One of his most notable pupils was Nelson Dawson (1859-1942), whose 1906 design for a candlestick is reproduced on p. 178. In common with other Arts and Crafts designers, Dawson was fascinated by the idea of the craft guild, and founded the Artificers' Guild in 1901 in his Chiswick workshop. His original watercolour, pen and pencil sketches are held in the Victoria & Albert Museum, London.

Archibald Knox brought an altogether more elegant touch to his designs for Liberty, transforming the swirls of 'Celtic' iconography into refined and elegant realizations of Arts and Crafts ideals in metal. This candlestick design (p. 179), probably for the Cymric range, has an engaging stylishness, yet is thoroughly modern and functional in its rectilinear central column and broad foot.

These watercolour and pencil designs by William De Morgan (see pp. 137 and 164-165) for vases date from 1880-84, roughly the period when the most eminent ceramist of the Arts and Crafts Movement was in closest contact with William Morris at Merton Abbey. Like Morris, De Morgan drew much of his decorative vocabulary directly from nature – leaves, animals and birds – and then deployed it with a vigour and clarity which sometimes rival the imaginative power of Morris's own designs. De Morgan was particularly adept at suiting motif to the form of any vessel, as in the case of the lizard designs here. In this, De Morgan was more designer than potter, often employing assistants to apply his designs to the wares.

In many ways, Christopher Dresser (see pp. 144-145) could be considered as one of the first professional designers in the modern sense. Unlike Morris and many of the Arts and Crafts designers and craftsmen associated with the guild movement, Dresser directly addressed the problems of providing good design for manufacture in industrial conditions. As early as the 1870s he was designing domestic artefacts in metal which seem to prefigure the modernist aesthetic of the Bauhaus. In 1879 he became the art director of the Linthorpe Pottery near Middlesbrough, producing designs for a variety of vessels and ornamental pieces. The bold, simple lines of his designs of this period, a page of which is reproduced here, reflect his admiration for the elegant minimalism of Japanese applied arts.

Unlike many of the great English retail businesses which burgeoned during the latter part of the nineteenth century to serve the needs of an increasingly wealthy middle class, the firm of Liberty was devoted to the purveying of fine design from its inception in 1875.

5

INTO ARTS *and* CRAFTS

Founded by Arthur Lasenby Liberty (1843-1917), its first trade was in fine artefacts from the East, but by the end of the century it was playing a central role in the dissemination of Arts and Crafts and Art Nouveau design, often in association with the leading designers of the day, including C.F.A. Voysey, Rex Silver and Archibald Knox. Both of the latter provided the firm with numerous designs for its 'Cymric' range of silverware and its 'Tudric' range of pewter, decorated with interpretations of 'Celtic' forms and floral and plant motifs. Attribution of the designs (like those for the silver wares reproduced here) is difficult, since Liberty's guarded the identity of their designers, several of whom worked in similar styles. The actual manufacture of the metalwork was undertaken by the firm of W.H. Haseler in Birmingham, but the Liberty catalogues simply note that it was made to 'Original Designs by Liberty & Co.' These pages are reproduced from a 350-page hand-bound volume containing drawings of a substantial amount of the Liberty product range, including bowls, clocks, dishes, decanters, mirrors, trays, tea sets and tankards.

pages 184–185

The Spode factory (see pp. 108, 112-113 and 126) continued to flourish throughout the latter half of the nineteenth century under the name of W.T. Copeland & Sons Ltd. These two pages, dating from *c.* 1880-90, are reproduced from a pattern book of 302 designs. The individual designs are on paper sheets which have been stitched to the cloth pages of the book. Such patterns would have been used for tiles or panels in furniture and fireplaces. In some cases designs were repeated in two record books, one version to be shown to the customer, the other to be retained as the factory production record.

pages 186–187

A timely reminder that the whole of English design for manufacture in the latter part of the nineteenth century was not imbued with the ideals of the Arts and Crafts Movement are these wooden mouldings offered in a trade catalogue of 1900 by Charrier & Marbut Carvings Ltd. These traditional designs for 'carved enrichments' were intended for 'builders and property developers.'

pages 188–189

Initially engaged in general commercial pottery, the firm of Thomas Twyford began to produce sanitaryware around 1850. By the time it was producing its 1883 'catalogue of earthenware sanitary goods', from which the reproductions on p. 188 are taken, the firm had been granted a royal warrant and had won many awards and medals; it also had agents in the United States, Germany, Austria, Switzerland, The Netherlands and Australia. The 1894 catalogue, from which the designs on p. 189 are taken, contains a number of variations on basic designs, including the engagingly named 'Deluge' flush lavatory.

pages 190–191

Archibald Knox (1864-1933) was probably one of the most prolific contributors of designs to Liberty's 'Cymric' and 'Tudric' ranges (see pp. 179 and 183) of metalwork. A relatively unsung master of the Arts and Crafts Movement in England, his work was exhibited with success on the Continent, notably in Germany. Indeed, these designs for his 'Forever, Never' clock have a

distinct affinity with those of the Darmstadt Jugendstil designers. The minute hand was intended to be in silver and that for the hour in mother-of-pearl.

pages 192–193

Like the wood mouldings illustrated on pp. 186-187, this page of ornamental masonry designs for windows and doorways from *The Illustrated Carpenter and Builder* of 17 April 1891 illustrates that the mainstream building and design industry was still very much beholden to historical references. Derived from classical models, the pediments and lintels and other features illustrated in this weekly tabloid are probably a much closer barometer of popular taste than the design aesthetic expressed in this sideboard (p. 193) from the firm of William Birch. This design may very well have been the original for pieces sold through Liberty's London shop.

page 194

Most commercial late Victorian design seems flaccid and unadventurous against the bold innovatory visions of

5
INTO ARTS
and
CRAFTS

Morris and De Morgan. Yet much of it is pleasant enough, as is this assembly of tile designs, showing the influence of the vision of the creative reformers of the latter part of the century. These designs are taken from a pattern book in the Victoria & Albert Museum, London: it has no introduction and bears no company name, although this may have been lost during later rebinding in the 1970s. The designs are printed one to a page in black but have been coloured by hand. The volume, probably intended for sales representatives, would have been printed in a small edition and disseminated among the manufacturers of such wares as fireplaces, wash-stands and other furniture.

page 195

Most closely associated with Edward Godwin (1833-86), the Aesthetic Movement was a powerful force in English art, literature, design and culture during the 1870s and 1880s. It was a self-conscious rejection of the values of the Victorian middle class in favour of an 'art for art's sake' approach to living. Interiors in the style tended to be relatively simple with a reliance on such

'aesthetic' colours as green and yellow, as in this example of 1878 by Walker & Sons for 8 Princes Gardens.

pages 196–201

Ornamental and tableware designs, probably for manufacture in silver, from the Liberty archive, in Westminster City Library; the heyday of the firm's silver venture ran from about 1900 to 1912, but many of these designs were still in production in the 1920s and 1930s. The 350-page pattern book from which these pages are reproduced is prefaced with a list of contents, including bowls, caddies, cruets, decanters, sugar tongs, tea sets and vases. The drawings are in pen and ink on ruled paper.

page 202

The Wedgwood factory continued the manufacture of what it termed 'majolica' until the latter part of the nineteenth century. This pattern for a 'Franklin Strawberry Set, brown ground' is recorded in the company archives (begun in 1760) as being from 1880.

page 203

As if to demonstrate the durability of the designs of William Morris, this pattern ('Fruit') in fact dates from the very early years of the company, although the production log from which this illustration is taken dates from 5 September 1910. This page, now separated from its binding, shows the three colourways of the pattern, along with the number of blocks (12) needed to print it. The aesthetics of Morris undoubtedly continued as a dominant influence on English design throughout the turn-of-the-century years of Arts and Crafts.

pages 204–205

The fireplace and chimneypiece had a peculiar fascination for Arts and Crafts designers, especially for those who tended to see the movement as a vehicle for reinterpreting the English vernacular. As a feature it dominated room settings and provided unique design opportunities. Ernest Gimson's undated sketch (p. 204) suggests some of the monumentality which characterized his furniture design. John Hungerford

Pollen's design (p. 205) for a fireplace at Blickling Hall seems to draw on a colder, grand-hall aspect of the English vernacular.

pages 206–207

The Silver Studio was one of the principal suppliers of textile designs to Liberty & Co. and many patterns which are thought of as being distinctly 'Liberty' in fact emanated from this group of designers. Notable among them was Harry Napper, the author of these two designs, who joined the studio *c.* 1893 and managed its production after the death of Arthur Silver in 1896. Like many Arts and Crafts designers, Napper turned his hand to other disciplines, including furniture and metalwork design.

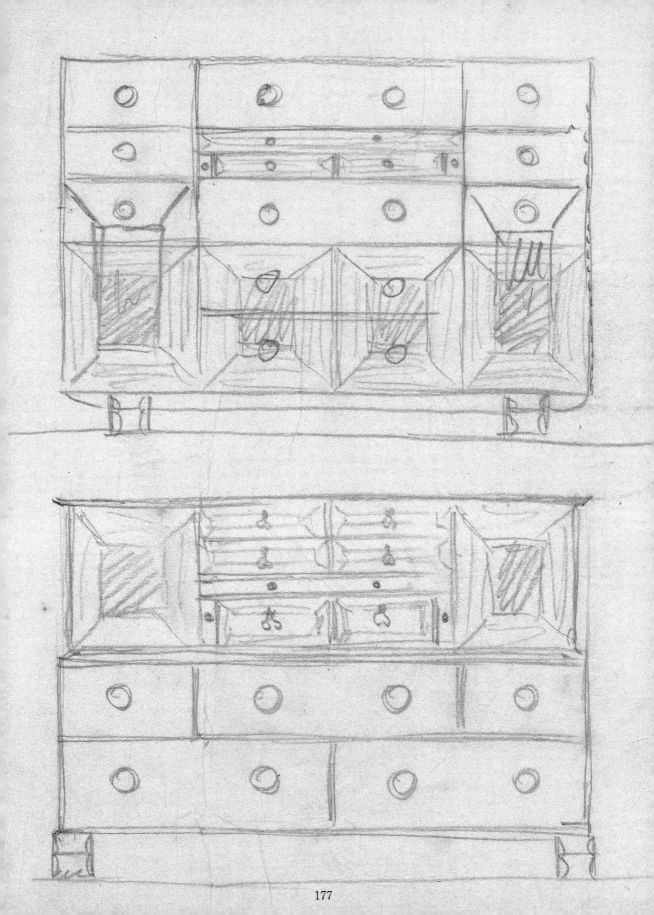

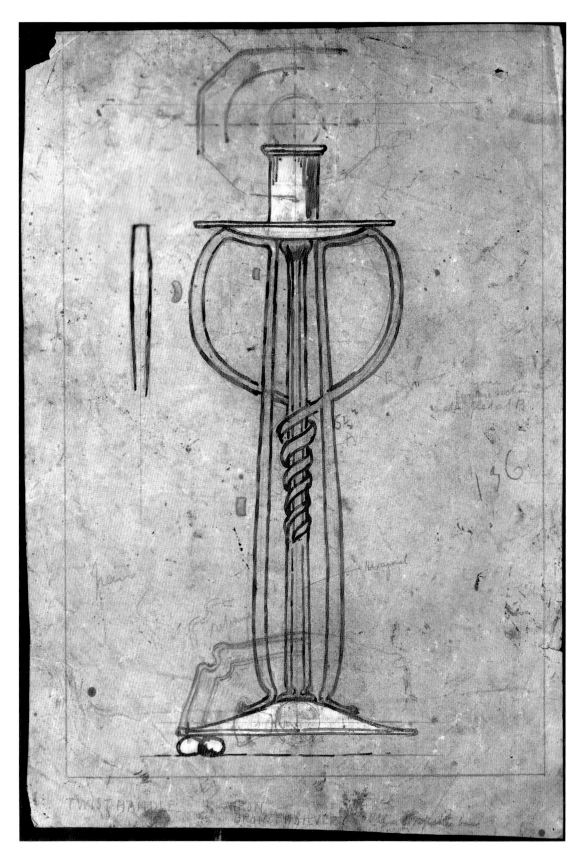

CANDLE STICK
circular base

179

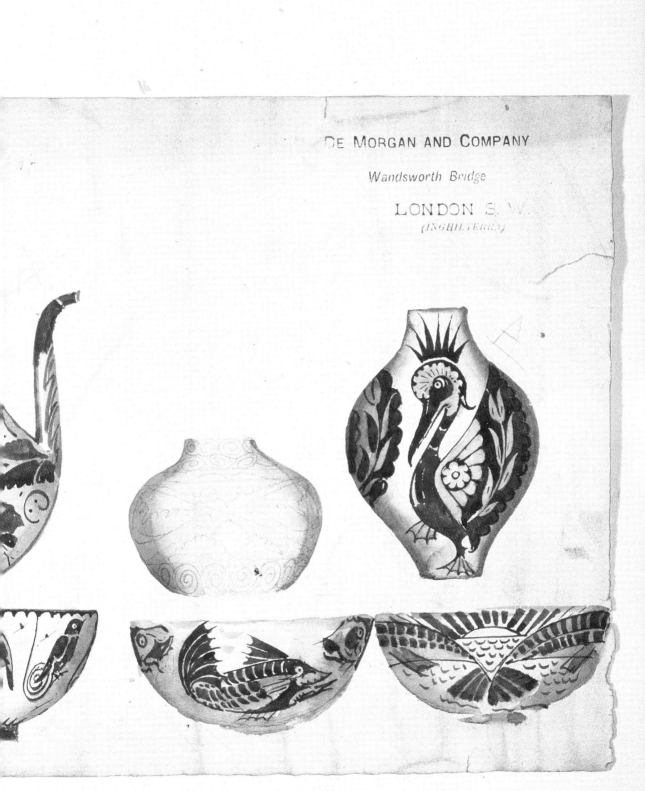

De Morgan and Company

Wandsworth Bridge

LONDON S. W.
(INGHILTERRA)

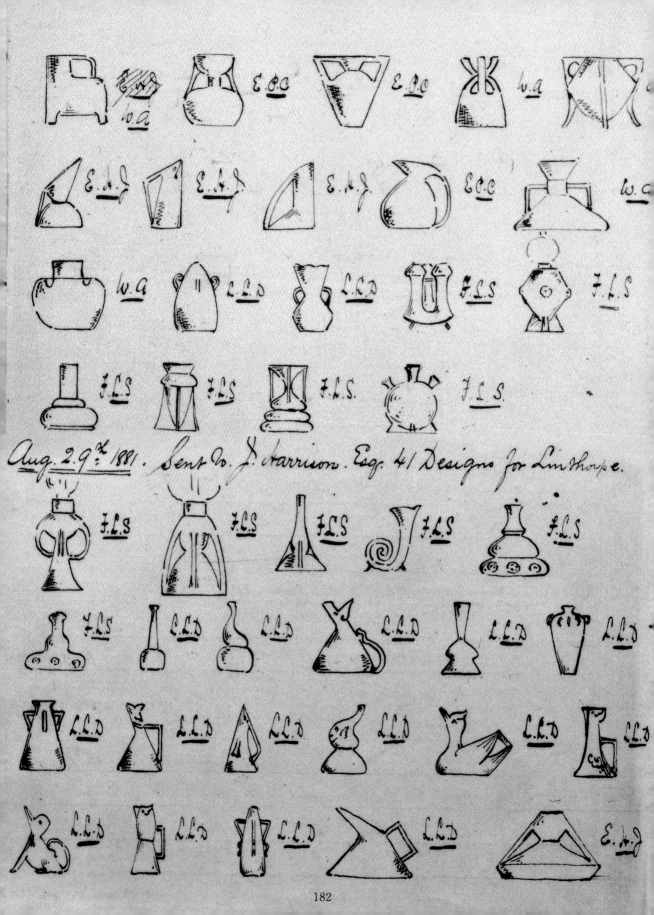

Aug. 29th 1881. Sent to J. Harrison. Esq. 41 Designs for Linthorpe.

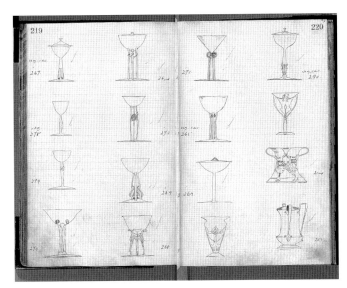

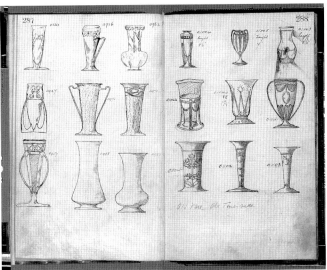

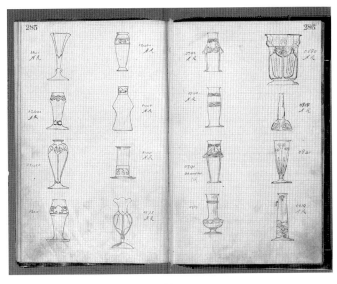

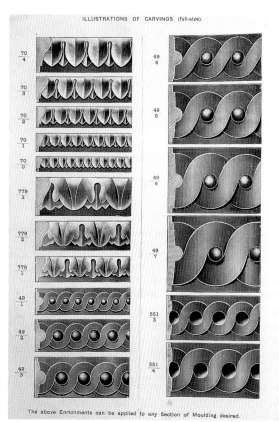

The above Enrichments can be applied to any Section of Moulding desired.

The above Enrichments can be applied to any Section of Moulding desired.

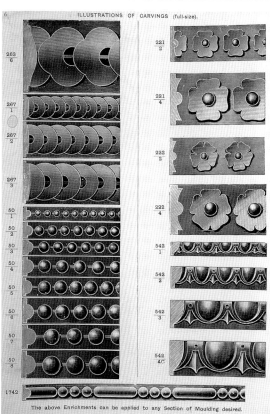

The above Enrichments can be applied to any Section of Moulding desired.

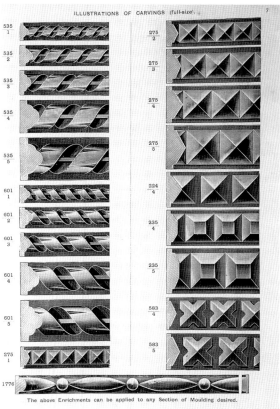

The above Enrichments can be applied to any Section of Moulding desired.

186

187

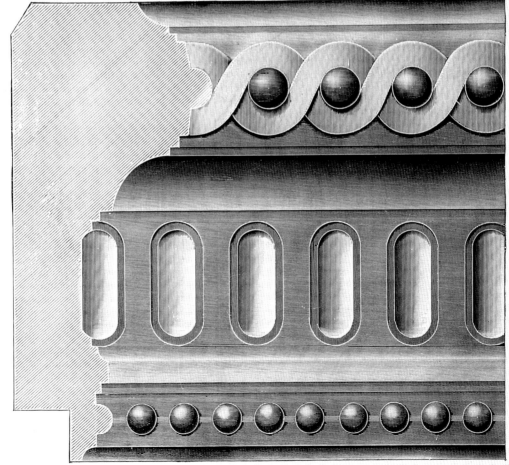

192

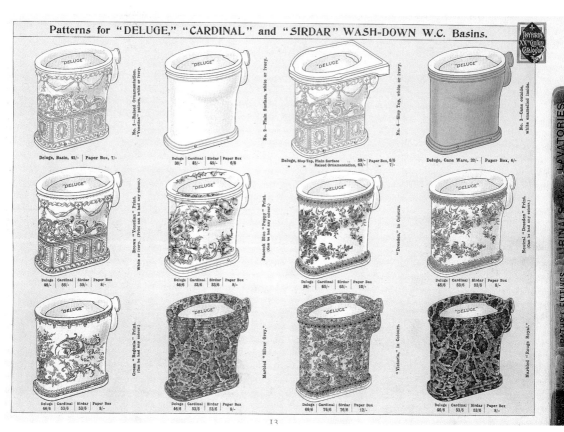

Patterns for "DELUGE," "CARDINAL" and "SIRDAR" WASH-DOWN W.C. Basins.

Deluge, Basin, 42/- | Paper Box, 7/-

No. 4—Raised Ornamentation, "Venetian" pattern, white or ivory.

Deluge	Cardinal	Sirdar	Paper Box
38/-	45/-	45/-	6/6

No. 2—Plain Surface, white or ivory.

| Deluge, Slop Top, Plain Surface | 59/- | Paper Box, 6/6 |
| " " Raised Ornamentation, 63/- | | 7/- |

No. 4—Slop Top, white or ivory.

Deluge, Cane Ware, 32/- | Paper Box, 6/-

No. 3—Cane outside, white enamelled inside.

Deluge	Cardinal	Sirdar	Paper Box
48/-	55/-	55/-	8/-

Brown "Venetian" Print. White or ivory. (Print can be had any colour.)

Deluge	Cardinal	Sirdar	Paper Box
46/6	53/6	53/6	8/-

Peacock Blue "Foggy" Print. (Can be had any colour.)

Deluge	Cardinal	Sirdar	Paper Box
58/-	65/-	65/-	10/-

"Dresden," in Colours.

Deluge	Cardinal	Sirdar	Paper Box
46/6	53/6	53/6	8/-

Neutral "Dresden" Print. (Can be had any colour.)

Deluge	Cardinal	Sirdar	Paper Box
46/6	53/6	53/6	8/-

Green "Begonia" Print. (Can be had any colour.)

Deluge	Cardinal	Sirdar	Paper Box
46/6	53/6	53/6	8/-

Marbled "Silver Grey."

Deluge	Cardinal	Sirdar	Paper Box
69/6	76/6	76/6	12/-

"Victoria," in Colours.

Deluge	Cardinal	Sirdar	Paper Box
46/6	53/6	53/6	8/-

Marbled "Rouge Royal."

13

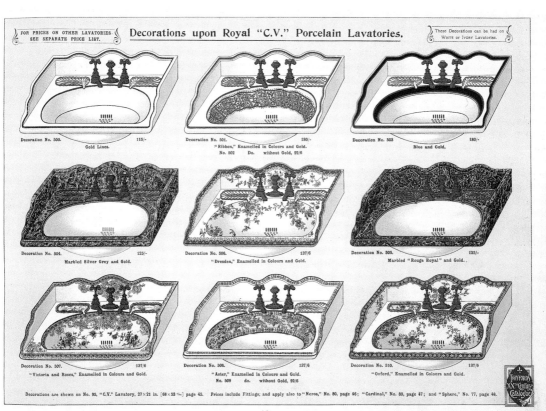

Decorations upon Royal "C.V." Porcelain Lavatories.

FOR PRICES ON OTHER LAVATORIES SEE SEPARATE PRICE LIST.

These Decorations can be had on WHITE or IVORY Lavatories.

Decoration No. 500.   115/-
Gold Lines.

Decoration No. 501.   180/-
"Ribbon," Enamelled in Colours and Gold.
No. 502   Do.   without Gold, 92/6

Decoration No. 503.   180/-
Blue and Gold,

Decoration No. 504.   125/-
Marbled Silver Grey and Gold.

Decoration No. 506.   137/6
"Dresden," Enamelled in Colours and Gold.

Decoration No. 505.   125/-
Marbled "Rouge Royal" and Gold.

Decoration No. 507.   137/6
"Victoria and Roses," Enamelled in Colours and Gold.

Decoration No. 508.   137/6
"Aster," Enamelled in Colours and Gold.
No. 509   do.   without Gold, 92/6

Decoration No. 510.   137/6
"Oxford," Enamelled in Colours and Gold.

Decorations are shown on No. 95, "C.V." Lavatory, 27×21 in. [68×53 %] page 45. Prices include Fittings; and apply also to "Neros," No. 80, page 46; "Cardinal," No. 89, page 47; and "Sphere," No. 77, page 48.

49

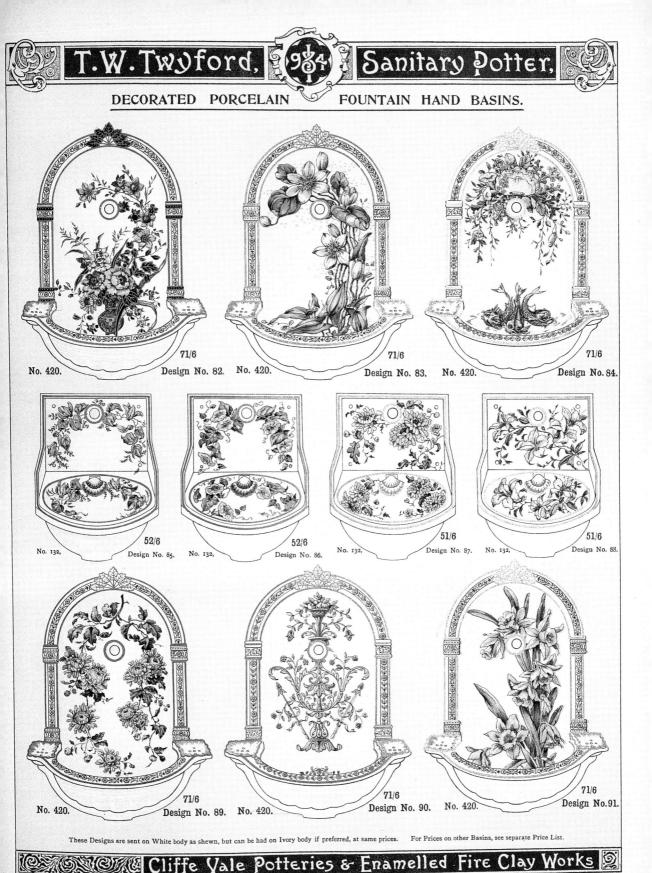

71/6
No. 420.   Design No. 82.

71/6
No. 420.   Design No. 83.

71/6
No. 420.   Design No. 84.

52/6
No. 132,   Design No. 85.

52/6
No. 132,   Design No. 86.

51/6
No. 132,   Design No. 87.

51/6
No. 132,   Design No. 88.

71/6
No. 420.   Design No. 89.

71/6
No. 420.   Design No. 90.

71/6
No. 420.   Design No. 91.

These Designs are sent on White body as shewn, but can be had on Ivory body if preferred, at same prices.   For Prices on other Basins, see separate Price List.

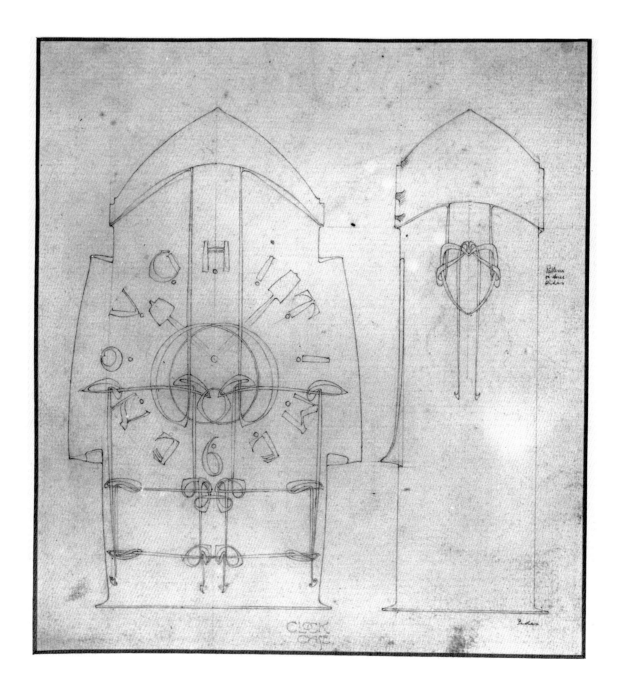

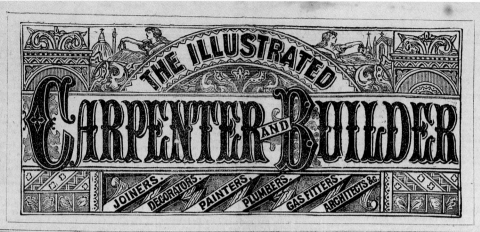

THE ILLUSTRATED CARPENTER AND BUILDER

JOINERS. DECORATORS. PAINTERS. PLUMBERS. GAS FITTERS. ARCHITECTS &c.

Vol. XXVIII.—No. 715.] Registered as a Newspaper.   FRIDAY, APRIL 17, 1891.   [Price One Penny.

ORNAMENTAL MASONRY: MOULDINGS FOR WINDOWS AND DOORWAYS.

CB 1906 15/m/

Nº 54   57   Nº 75

Nº 800   Nº 63

Nº A2   R ¼ Nº 65700   Nº F   Nº A5

Nº M   Nº 81

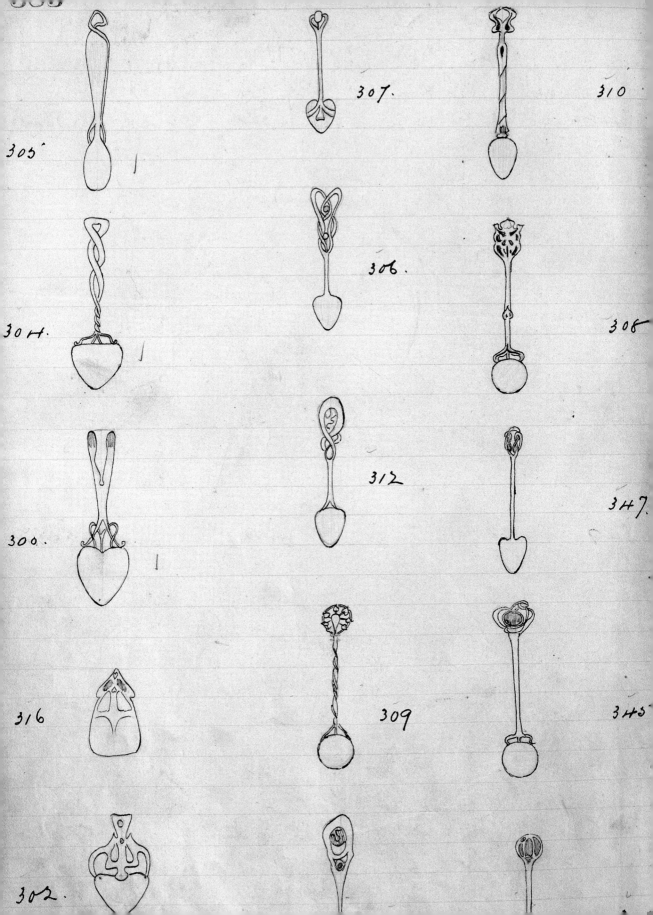

305

307.

310

304.

306.

308

300.

312

347.

316

309

345

302.

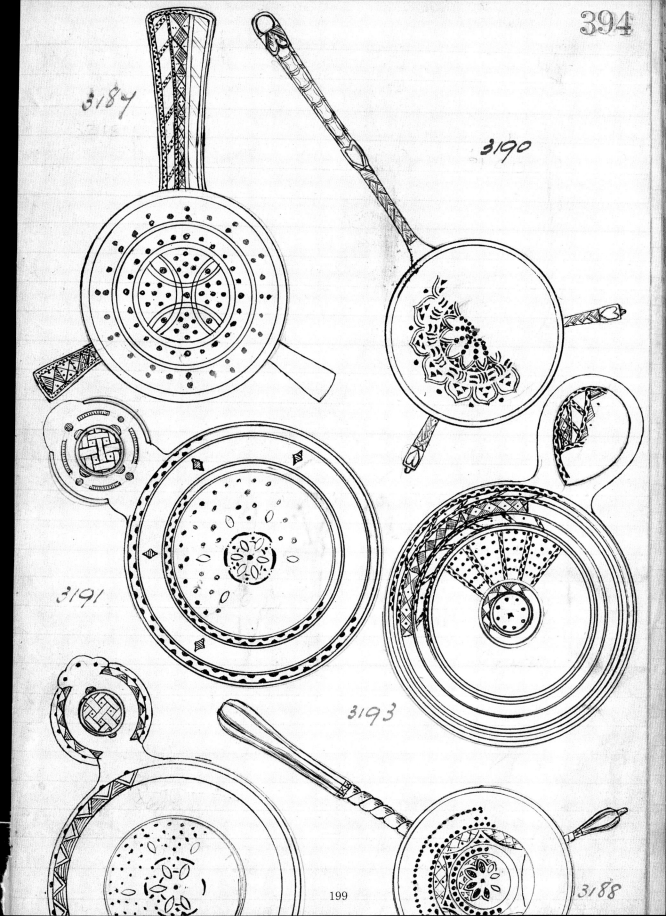

3187

3190

3191

3193

3188

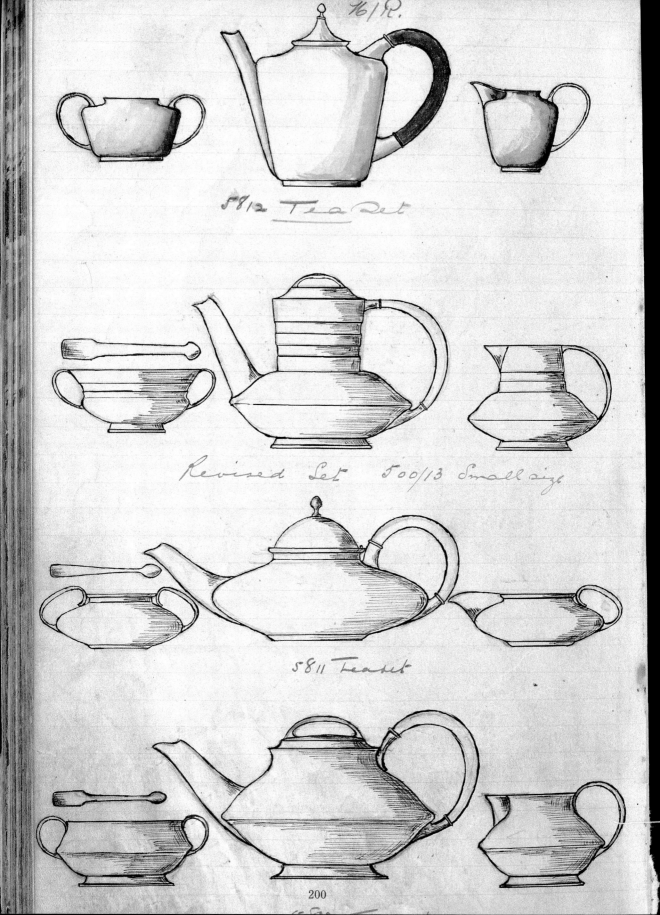

5812 Tea Set

Revised Set   500/13 Small size

5811 Teaset

5821 Cream Sugar & Tongs

5815

4 3/8 Lip to handle

Tea Dia.

5827

5814

Coffee Pot on page 418

No 2996 Franklin strawberry brown ground see pattern

Flowers
White

Celeste

Celeste

Green
Yellow
and
Crimson

Handle
in
Rockingham
Brown

No 2997 Franklin strawberry and celeste ground

Blue

Handles a
No 2996

03594

N°03082.

raditionalism *to* MODERNISM

The very success of the Arts and Crafts

Movement led in the twentieth century to a relative decline in English design, mainly because it failed signally to address the problems of machine production and the new aesthetic associated with it. None of the major art schools provided training in design for mass manufacture. Even the Central School of Art, founded by W.R. Lethaby in 1896, which enjoyed a reputation throughout Europe for teaching progressive design theory, still drew heavily on the craft-orientated and anti-manufacturing thinking of the disciples of William Morris. The Design and Industries Association of 1915, whose founder members included Ambrose Heal, also retained many of the hallowed Arts and Crafts values, even though its avowed purpose was to improve the design of manufactured goods for domestic use.

In furniture design the legacy of the nineteenth-century reformers was continued by such as Ambrose Heal and Gordon Russell. Catalogues of the 'twenties and 'thirties show a selection of well-crafted but 'safe' pieces which now looked deeply conservative in comparison with production in Scandinavia and Germany and distinctly drab if set beside the magnificent creations exhibited at the 1925 Paris Exposition, dominated by Ruhlmann, Süe et Mare and Lalique. Liberty's turn-of-the-century catalogues show a similar continuation of Arts and Crafts styles in sturdy oak and mahogany pieces interspersed with ladder-back and slatted chairs resembling the productions of the Cotswold School.

TRADITIONALISM *to* MODERNISM

Indeed, Gimson and the Barnsleys continued to exercise considerable influence over English furniture design, along with their Dutch associate Peter Waals, who continued the production of Cotswold craft furniture until 1937.

 n textile production Liberty's characteristic patterns of the late nineteenth century continued in production, but new design concentrated very much on a nostalgic English country style in the form of floral chintzes. But in a corner of Bloomsbury a more adventurous aesthetic was being applied to textiles and other articles of household use. The Omega Workshops (Artist Decorators) were founded by artists closely affiliated to the Bloomsbury Group, including Duncan Grant, Vanessa Bell, Wyndham Lewis and Edward Wadsworth, under the leadership of the art critic Roger Fry. Their gallery opened in Fitzroy Square in July 1913 to sell painted furniture, hand-dyed textiles, pottery and other items. In spite of a professed modernism and the application of abstract design, however, Omega always retained a slightly homespun air and its productions remained craft-based. But one of its artists, Wyndham Lewis (whose designs are reproduced on pp. 236 and 244–245), did develop a tougher, more aggressive style, much more suitable to modernist environments and interiors than the rather self-consciously charming colour schemes and patterns of Grant and Bell.

 nd modernism did eventually make itself known in British design. In ceramics the dominant British art tradition had always been that of the craft-based studio potter, exemplified by Bernard Leach and William Staite-Murray. But in commercial production, the twenties designs of Clarice Cliff and Susie Cooper showed a new boldness in colour and form which was distinctly modern.

 he kind of geometric, angular modernism of Cliff and early Cooper gradually came to be found in other types of design. Individual furniture designers working out of exclusive premises began to emerge to cater for the few, while the less privileged were learning the advantages of built-in, standardized furniture for a generation of smaller houses and flats. A less individual age of design had arrived.

page 208 It seems appropriate to begin this twentieth-century chapter with a 1926 design by C.F.A. Voysey (1857-1941). A versatile designer of houses and furniture, who looked back to Pugin and Morris as influences, Voysey nevertheless continued to design well into the twentieth century and is sometimes claimed as one of the first modernists. In addition to his three-dimensional work, he was a prolific designer of flat patterns for tiles, wallpapers, fabrics, rugs and carpets; this pattern was for a carpet by Tomkinson's of Kidderminster.

right F. Austin's furniture factory in Lea Bridge Road, London, 1936; a photograph taken for *The Cabinet Maker*.

6

TRADITIONALISM *to* MODERNISM

pages 212-213

This modernist interior by Paul Nash (1889-1948) (see pp. 238-239) was first published in *The Studio* yearbook for 1930 after gaining second prize in a competition to design an apartment for Lord Benbow. The assessor's report, in its attempts to understand the modernist aesthetic, makes fascinating reading: 'The second prize has been awarded to a design which is made faintly ridiculous by the fact that the artist either misunderstood the purport of the remarks regarding Lord Benbow's sporting tastes, or deliberately surrendered to his sense of humour… At the same time, in the assessor's opinion this design shows a truer architectural quality than any other submitted. It is placed second because it is less successful than the winning design in exploiting the particular idiosyncrasies of Lord Benbow's plan. Taking very simple motifs, like the thin cylindrical light fittings and the square frames of picture and partition, it builds up by means of combination, repetition, and contrast a subtle fugue-like organization in which the planes of the walls play their part. The interplay of incident, the feeling for volume, the cunning punctuation provided by the dark bodies, is intellectually agreeable.'

page 217

Some of Voysey's later work (see p. 208) seems to run counter to the clean, bold lines of his turn-of-the-century furniture and architecture. This 'Ten Fruits' design from the Tomkinson Carpets archive, dated May 1926, was never actually put into manufacture and may have been originally intended as a wallpaper pattern. It is strikingly similar to a 1929 design for chintz, 'The House that Jack Built'.

pages 218-219

Like Voysey, Ernest Gimson (1864-1919) continued to produce designs in an Arts and Crafts idiom until well into the twentieth century. His partnership with the Barnsley brothers (both of whom lived on until 1926) appears to have dissolved in 1904, and from then on Gimson concentrated very much on design rather than on the practical aspects of making furniture. Many of the architectural sketches in the archives of the Cheltenham Art Gallery and Museums date from this period, and show a persistent affection for the English rustic vernacular, drawing on medieval models for the positioning of uprights and beams (p. 218) and even for overall layout (p. 219).

pages 220-221

Although Gimson stuck very much to his Arts and Crafts ideals in his twentieth-century work, a certain rectilinearity, more in keeping with the aesthetic of the new century, does appear in some of his later work. This bold, simple approach to furniture-making was continued by the Dutch cabinet-maker Peter Waals who went on to employ a number of Gimson's craftsmen after the death of Gimson in 1919. These undated sketches for 'Washstands & dressing tables with bright steel of brass handles. Chests-of-drawers' are executed in pencil and watercolour on tracing paper.

pages 222-223

One famous characteristic of Gimson's furniture design was his intense regard for the value and suitability of the varied woods and materials he used. Each had a distinct part to play in what were sometimes patterns and structures of great complexity. This cabinet (p. 222), for instance, is described as being in ebony (the 'brown' has been deleted) and English walnut with gilt gesso panels in black ebony; the stand is also in black ebony. This use of contrasting exotic woods, it has been suggested, anticipates the luxury furniture design of the French Art Deco masters in the 1920s. Even such an apparently simple design as that for a chair (p. 223) is deceptive; intended as the model for a set of six, it was to be made 'in ebony and burr elm on Honduras with stuffed leather seat'.

pages 224-225

The archive of the Whitefriars Glasshouse (James Powell & Sons) is a fascinating commentary on the creative process which leads to eventual manufacture. One of Harry Powell's notebooks dating from the turn of the century, from which these six pages are reproduced (p. 224) contains sketches and photographic records of designs and artefacts which could serve as inspiration for the making of glassware. These include a bottle from

1509, a silver-gilt chalice with enamel by Alexander Fisher, and a reproduction of an elephant carving from the choir stalls of Exeter Cathedral. One form entered in the book appears to be the likely inspiration for the pair of vase designs in the pattern book for 1903-10 (p. 225). This latter document is in fact a large ledger, possibly begun on 1 December 1903, although later amendments mention 1925-26. The designs, of both table and ornamental glass, are mainly executed in pencil, some with wash. Each one has a catalogue number and a letter to denote the type of glass. These two vase designs, which were intended for manufacture either in blue with sea-green 'tears' or in sea-green with blue 'tears', are similar to a less elongated version accompanied by the comment, 'Taken from a picture by Hugo van der Goes in the Uffizi Gallery.'

page 226

After the earnestness of Arts and Crafts, a note of colour and frivolity was brought to English design by the Omega Workshops. Founded in 1913 by the art critic Roger Fry in association with the artists Duncan Grant, Vanessa Bell, Wyndham Lewis and Henri Gaudier-Brezska, the workshop made painted furniture and ceramics and hand-dyed textiles. Unlike much of the production of the Arts and Crafts workshops, however, Omega artefacts were often shoddily made and are really only significant

because of their decoration. In the year following their opening, the workshops undertook the complete interior design of the Cadena Café at 59 Westbourne Grove, Bayswater, London, including the wall and ceiling decoration, furniture design, and even the design of the waitress's uniforms. Rugs to this design by Roger Fry were placed under each table. The Omega symbol appears in the original design but was omitted from the rugs which were actually placed in the café.

page 227

Described as being in 'the German modern style', this rug design from the Tomkinson archive does demonstrate that the modernist aesthetic had begun to influence English manufacture in the 1930s. Tomkinson's design director of the time, J.P. Bland, employed a staff of about forty, most of whom would have been engaged in turning out traditional designs. Nevertheless, their work was seen as being essentially 'art'; even as recently as 1969, the design staff still worked standing at easels.

pages 228-229

Tomkinson's carpet factory was originally established in Kidderminster, the heart of the English carpet-making region, in 1869, with its own design studio under the direction of a Mr. Cunningham. The company's design archive now

consists of over 10,000 original paintings on paper. Records also include a photographic log of every design and its specification. This 1930s design was produced by a member of the studio staff for manufacture as a high-quality stair carpet. The design is painted on two pieces of white cartridge paper measuring 36 inches by 30 inches and dated '23.3.39'. Calibrations marked at the edge of the design indicate the spool settings so that they could be loaded into the loom in the correct order.

page 230

From its foundation in the eighteenth century (see pp. 74-75, 148-149 and 203), the firm of Wedgwood has shown a willingness to adapt to changing circumstances. During the twentieth century, accordingly, it has been associated with some of the most innovative designers of ceramics, as well as continuing to manufacture its more traditional ware. Notable among the firm's rich and varied output for the first part of the twentieth century was the nursery ware of Susannah Margaretta (Daisy) Makeig-Jones (1881-1945), whose 'Golliwog' pattern is illustrated here. Daisy Makeig-Jones joined the Wedgwood factory, then based at Etruria, in 1909 and was given a permanent position there in 1911. She began to design tableware under the direction of resident artist James Hodgkins, her first lustre wares going into

production in 1915, continuing until 1931. Between 1916 and 1923 she produced a number of colourful nursery-ware patterns, including 'Chicken', 'Thumbelina', 'Cobble Bead and Zoo', 'Golliwog' and 'Yellow Stone Zoo'; she is perhaps best known for her 'Fairyland' and 'Ordinary' ranges of lustre ware. The 'Golliwog' pattern is entered in the factory records as number AK6580 and first recorded in May 1916. Its description reads, 'AK6580. Cream colour earthenware. Concave (shape). Golliwog printed in black underglaze, coloured underglaze in green, imperial violet, crimson, orange, brown, see-saw blue. Black line.'

page 231

These unattributed designs for ceramics are taken from albums dated c. 1912-20 now held by the Victoria & Albert Museum, London. Each design in the album is numbered and all are coloured by hand, but there is no mention of the designer's or manufacturer's name. The lack of the latter is strange and tantalizing, since the albums would have been used by the company as a record of designs available, most of which show floral and geometric decoration for plates, teapots, coffee pots, dishes and elegant jugs.

pages 232-233

The most eminent of the English lady potters of the first

part of the twentieth century, Clarice Cliff (1899-1972), started work in the lithography department at A.J. Wilkinson's earthenware factory in the town of Middleport in the Potteries in 1916. After four years she was transferred to the general decorating shop to work alongside Wilkinson's top designers, John Butler and Fred Ridgeway. By 1923 she was producing pieces bearing her own name - mainly figures of Indians or Arabs in a naïve style. The same naïveté can be seen in most of the sketches in this book, now lodged in the Hanley Library in Stoke-on-Trent. However, towards the back of the large-format scrapbook, which probably dates from the late 1920s, designs known as the 'Bizarre' range - first introduced in 1928 - begin to emerge. Though initially used as a colourful way of disguising inferior shapes, the range became more successful than anybody could have imagined and, by 1930, used Cliff's own shapes inspired by designs she had encountered in Paris.

pages 234-235

The reputation of Susie Cooper (1902-95) as an innovative designer now stands almost as high as that of Clarice Cliff; indeed, her many devotees would claim that she was the finer artist. These two pages, from one of two Cooper pattern books now lodged in the Wedgwood Museum archive, show earthenware entries E503-E506, dating from the 1930s. In an attempt to

establish her own style, Cooper set up her own pottery in the Chelsea Works, Moorland Road, Burslem, which she rented from Doulton & Co. from April 1930. She employed ten paintresses and was initially obliged to decorate blanks which she purchased from a variety of sources, including Doultons and Wood & Sons in Burslem where, in 1931, she moved the production and where she remained and indeed flourished until a fire in 1957. Susie Cooper Ltd., latterly a partner of R.H. & S.L. Plant, became a member of the Wedgwood group in March 1966, but undoubtedly her most creative period was during the 1930s.

pages 236-237

The association of Percy Wyndham Lewis (1884-1957) with the Omega Workshops was short-lived and he parted company with the rest of the group in 1914 to form his own Rebel Art Centre. This design of 1913 for a folding screen (p. 236) was one of the very few he produced under the Omega aegis. His style was altogether more aggressive and self-consciously modernist than the light, decorative designs of such as Duncan Grant (p. 237), whose pleasant, Post-Impressionist style was much more in keeping with the Omega ethos. Indeed, the break with Lewis was the result of a disagreement over the design for a Post-Impressionist room which Omega had been commissioned to contribute to

the *Daily Mail* Ideal Home Exhibition. The Grant design in watercolour is typical of the many he executed for Omega and was intended as a model for a domestic mural and door panels. It is not clear whether any eventual application would have been more precisely detailed.

pages 238-239

Best known as a painter, Paul Nash also designed glassware, tableware and domestic interiors (see pp. 212-213), including the famous bathroom for the dancer Tilly Losch in 1932. This design, however, is his only known foray into theatre sets; it was created for a one-act play, *The Truth About the Russian Dancers*, which J.M. Barrie had written specially for the ballerina Tamara Karsavina. The play, with music by Arnold Bax, was first performed on 15 March 1920 at the London Colosseum and revived six years later at the Savoy.

pages 240-241

These sketches for 'Moderne' light fittings are taken from a 460-page scrapbook of designs by A.C. Adamson, part of a bequest made by the designer to the National Art Library, Archive of Art and Design, held by the Victoria & Albert Museum, London. Adamson, whose designs show extraordinary variety of form within a generally Streamline Moderne idiom,

worked for the firm of Osler & Faraday from 1922, creating fittings for public buildings, churches and private houses.

pages 242-243

Omega pottery shapes, probably designed by Roger Fry; he was the only member of the Omega Workshops group to persevere with the design of new shapes rather than the decoration of existing 'blanks'. In 1914 he worked at Carter & Co.'s pottery in Dorset, where he made a prototype dinner service - plates, vases, and tea and coffee sets, so that moulds could be made, and larger quantities produced. In the Omega catalogue Fry proclaimed that pottery was 'essentially a form of sculpture', and intended that products made from the moulds should reproduce the irregularities of his originals.

pages 244-245

These four black-and-white designs for lampshades by Wyndham Lewis were lithographed in 1913. The products, part of an extensive collection of decorative furnishing objects, were probably among those shown by the Omega Workshop. Following a six-week exhibition on twentieth-century art held the next year at the Whitechapel Gallery and attended by 53,000 visitors, Roger Fry noted that the group had finally begun to show a small profit.

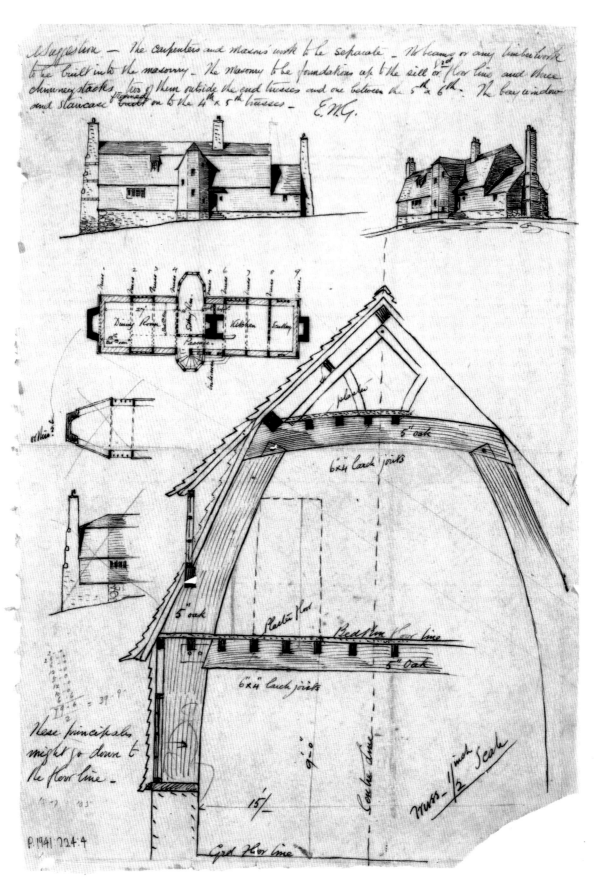

A Suggestion — The carpenters and masons' work to be separate — No beams or any timberwork to be built into the masonry — The masonry to be foundations up to the sill or 1st floor line and three chimney stacks, two of them outside the end trusses and one between the 5th & 6th. The bay window and staircase framed & built on to the 4th & 5th trusses — E.M.G.

Dining Room

Kitchen

Scullery

Passage

5" oak

6x4 larch joists

plaster

5" oak

plaster floor

Bed Room Floor line

5" oak

6x4 larch joists

These principals might go down to the floor line —

= 39' 9"

15'

Mess. ½ inch Scale

Centre line

9'-0

Grd. Floor line

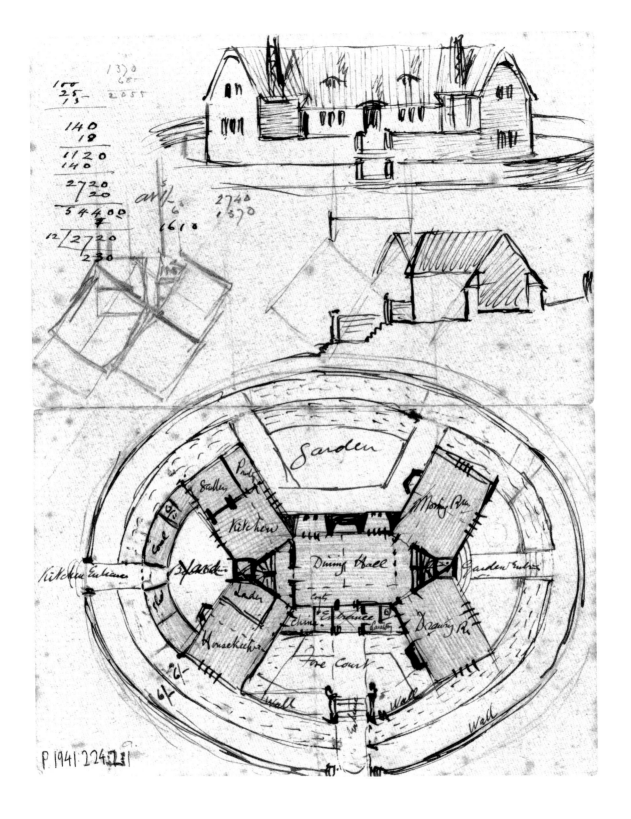

Garden

Studies

Pantry

Kitchen

Morning Room

Coal

Larder

Dining Hall

Kitchen Entrance

Garden Entrance

Larder

China

Entrance

Lavatory

Drawing Rm

Housekeeper

Fore Court

Wall

Wall

Wall

P. 1941.224.1.1

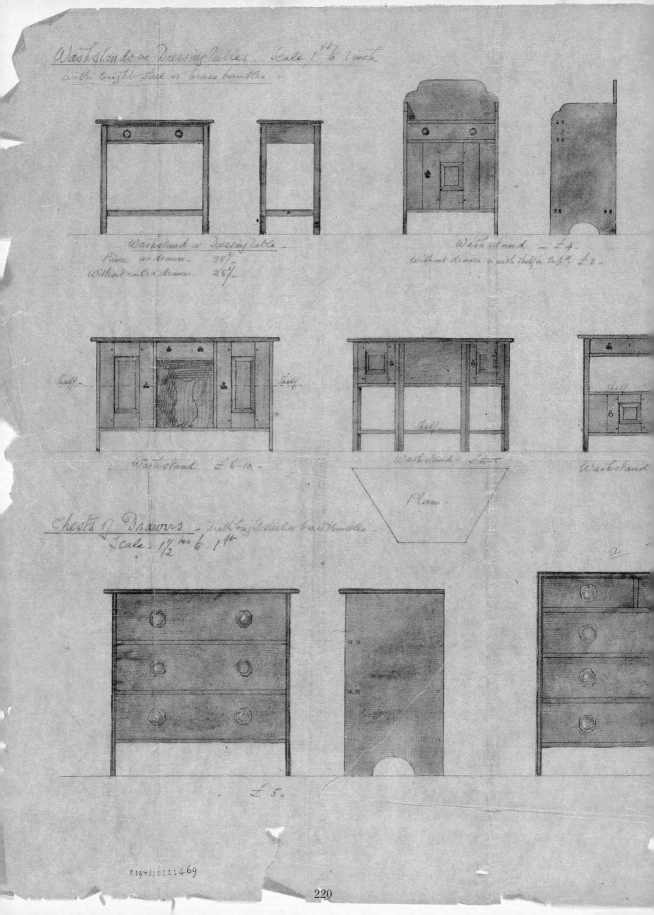

Washstands or Dressing Tables. Scale 1 ft to 1 inch
with bright steel or brass handles —

Washstand or Dressing Table.
Price as drawn. 35/-
Without rail & a drawer 28/-

Washstand — £4 —
Without drawer & with shelf on left £3 —

Washstand £6-10 —

Washstand — £5 —

Plan.

Washstand

Chests of Drawers — with bright steel or brass handles —
Scale: 1½ ins to 1 ft

£5 —

Corner   Washstand   Washstand or Dressing Table — £6.15.   End —
           £4.   Without drawers. £5.

Plan.

Shelf.

£3.10   Washstand £6.10   Washstand or Dressing Table £5.10.
                            without cross braces.   £5.

Plan.

Cupd with raised panel.

£6.10.   £9
                 with 5 drawers as above £8

Ernest W. Gimson

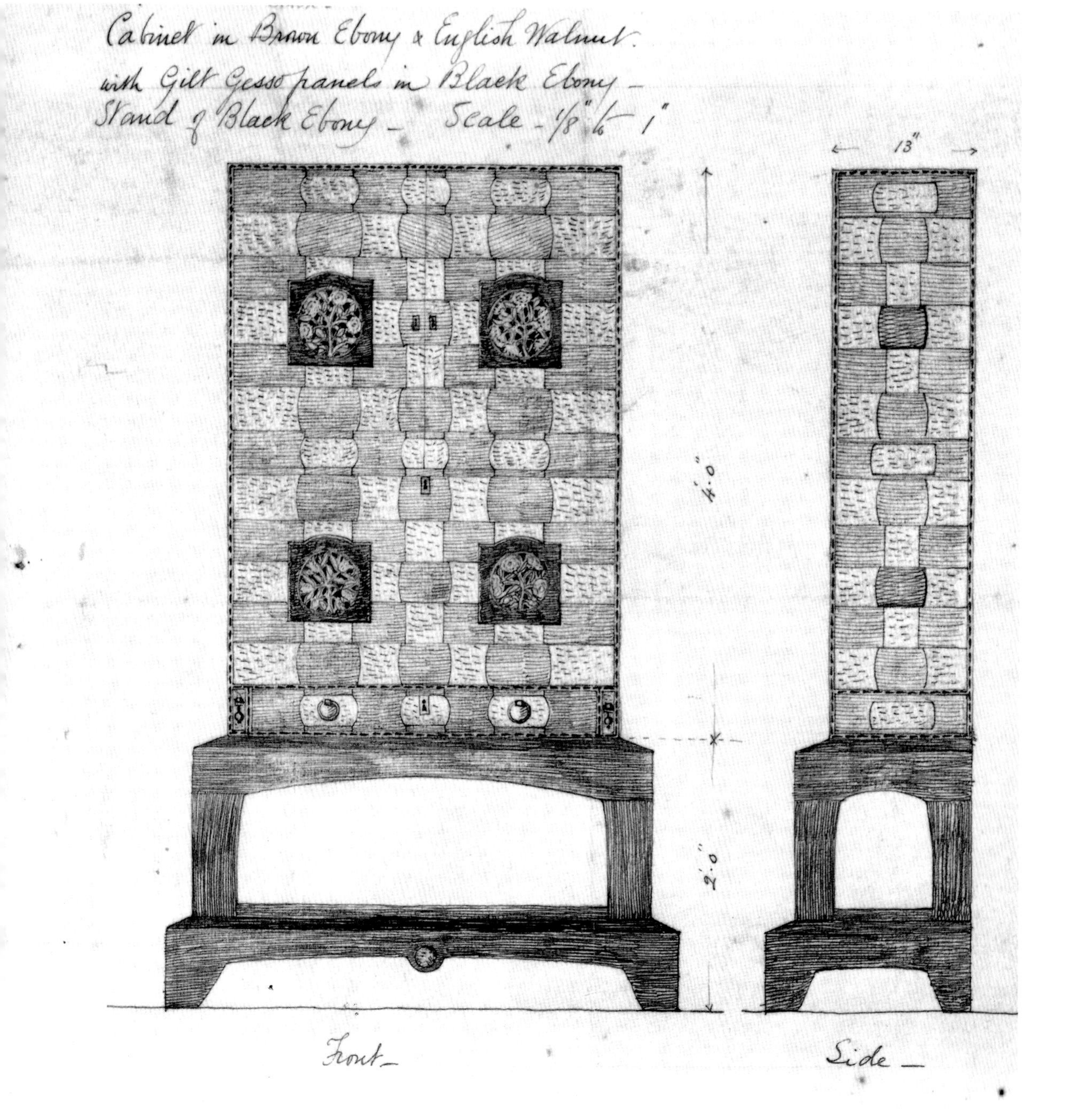

Cabinet in Brown Ebony & English Walnut.
with Gilt Gesso panels in Black Ebony —
Stand of Black Ebony —   Scale - 1/8" to 1"

13"

4'.0"

2'.0"

Front —   Side —

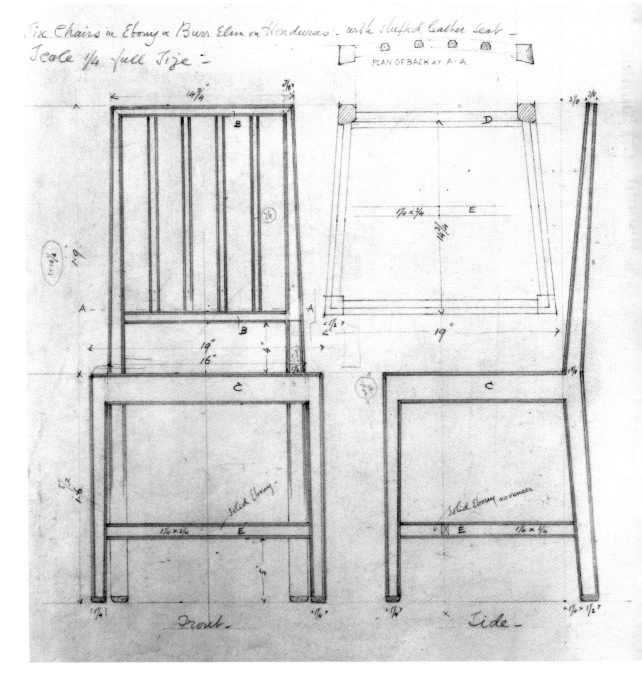

Six Chairs in Ebony & Burr Elm or Honduras - with stuffed Leather seat -
Scale 1/4 full Size :-

PLAN OF BACK AT A·A

14¾" 2⅛"

B

7/8

1·9

A

B

19"
16"

4"
½"

C

1¼ × ¾   E

Solid Ebony -

5

1¼"   ¼"

Front.

D

2⅛ 7/8

1¼ × ¾   E
3¼
14¼

½"

19"

15/8

C

Solid Ebony veneer

E   1¼ × ¾

¼   ¼   1⅛ × 1½"

Side -

223

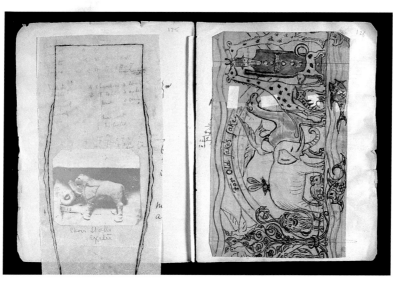

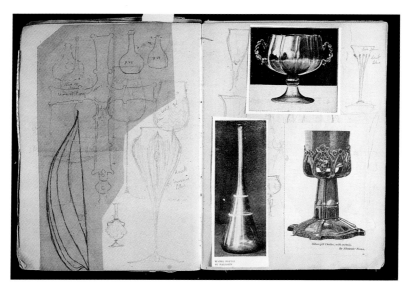

Flint milk blue n sea green tears

1106
a 9/-
B 10/-
C 11/3

Sea green milk blue tears

M.6
5.11

Coque
25/3/03

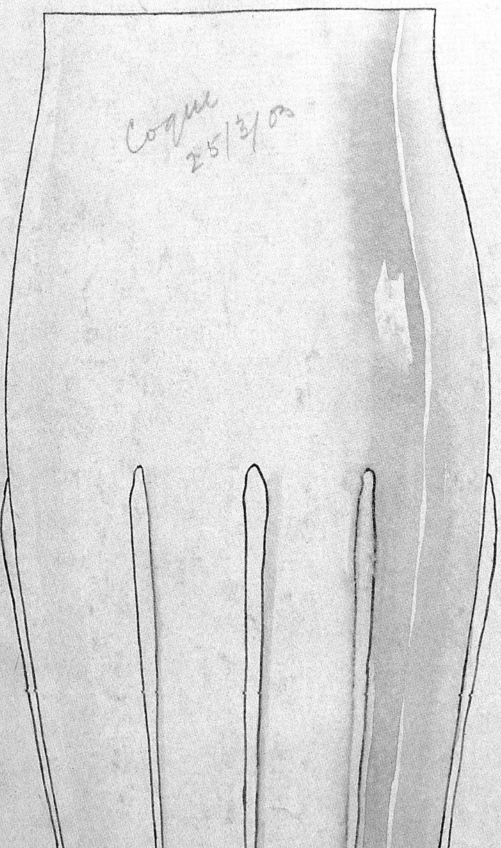

1107
a 7/6   7/-   14
B 8/3   7/9   15/6
C 9/6   8/9   17/6

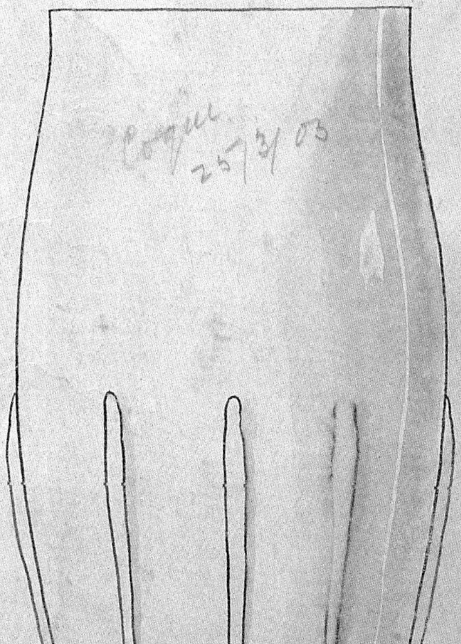

Coque
25/3/03

8 tears

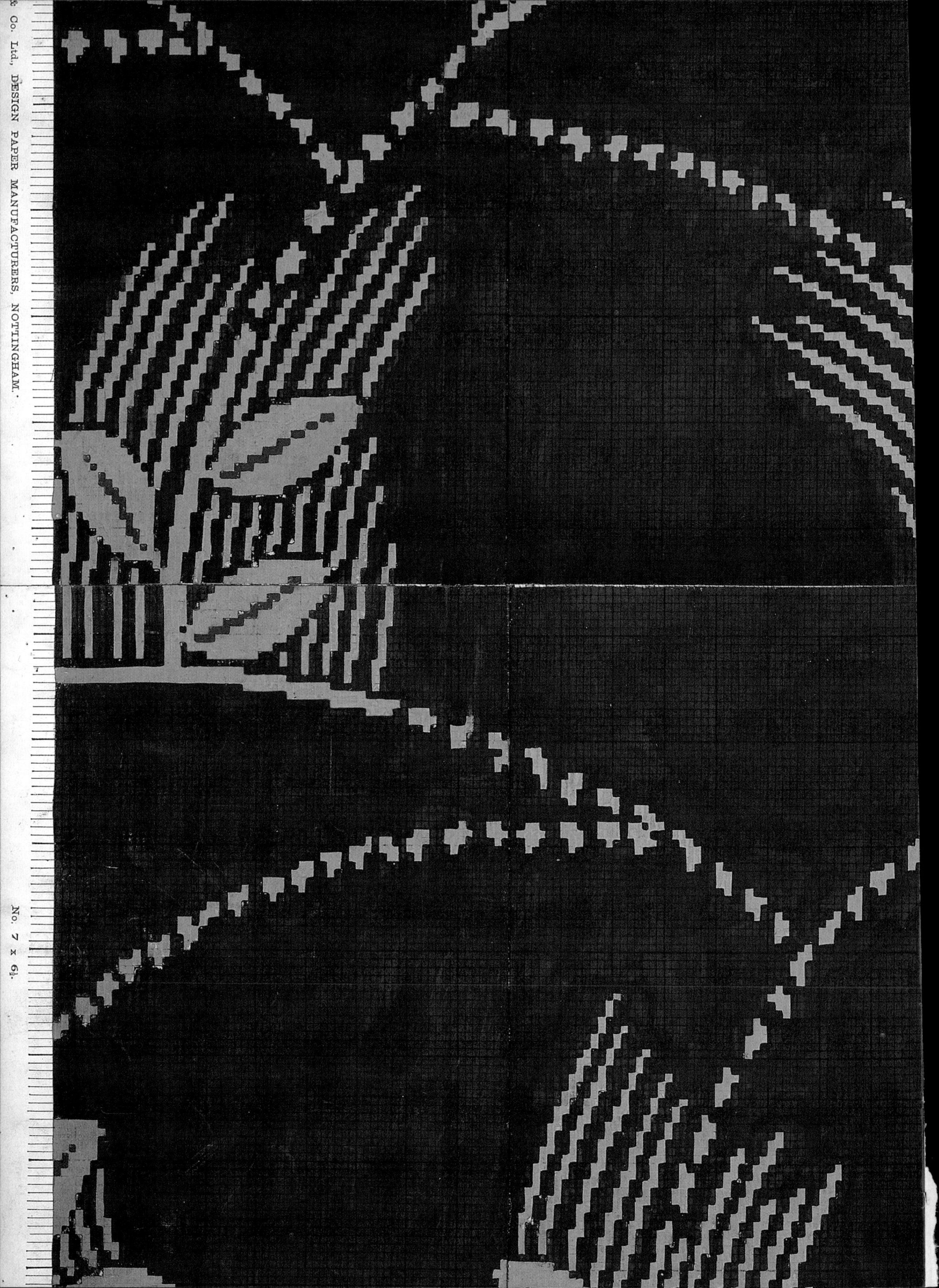
& Co. Ltd, DESIGN PAPER MANUFACTURERS, NOTTINGHAM.
No. 7 x 6¼

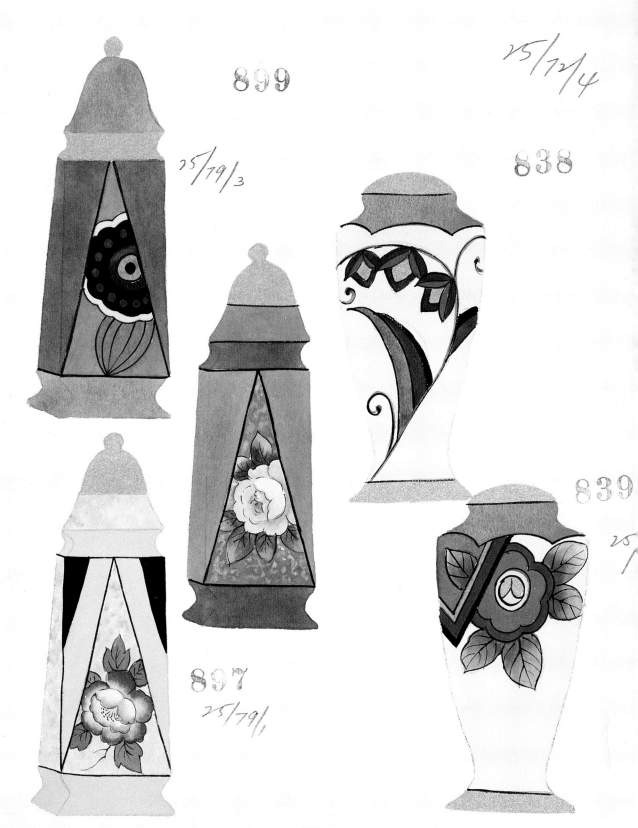

899

25/17/4

25/19/3

838

897

25/79/1

839

25/

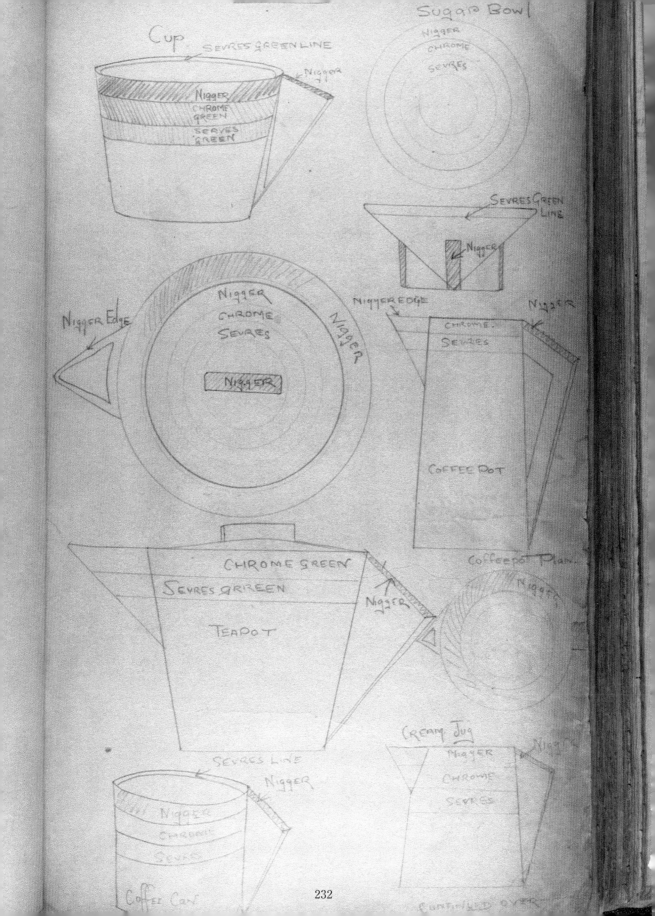

Cup.   SEVRES GREEN LINE

Nigger
Nigger
CHROME
GREEN
SEVRES
GREEN

Sugar Bowl

Nigger
CHROME
SEVRES

SEVRES GREEN Line

Nigger

Nigger

Nigger Edge

Nigger
CHROME
SEVRES

Nigger

NIGGER EDGE

Nigger

CHROME
SEVRES

COFFEE POT

Coffeepot Plan

Nigger

CHROME GREEN

SEVRES GREEN

Nigger

TEAPOT

Nigger

SEVRES LINE

Nigger

Nigger
CHROME
SEVRES

Coffee Can

Cream Jug

Nigger
Nigger
CHROME
SEVRES

CONTINUED OVER

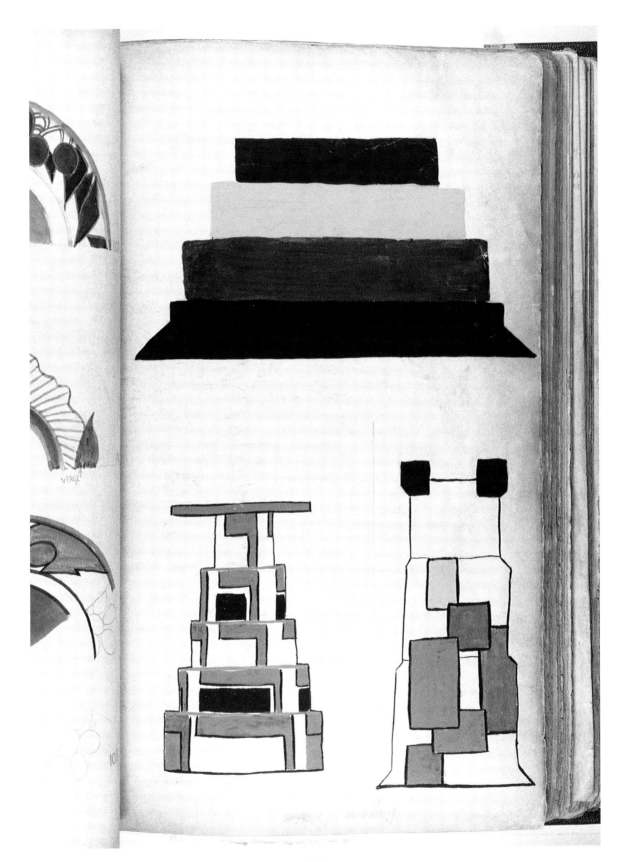

Conventional Floral Design in
Blythe Mixed Grey, Emerys Hair Brown,
Harrisons Tangerine and Emerys Purple
Brown.
No edge.
E503   Handle, black, solid.

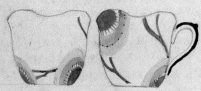
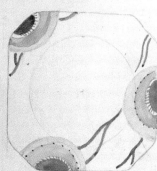

E504

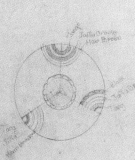

Geometrical Design. Ares in lines of
Colmans Jaffa Orange, Tangerine,
Hair Brown and Black.
Centre of saucer solid tangerine with black
scalloped band on verge.
Cups. 4 inch band from top inside.
Black scallop

Leaf Pattern in light Mixed Green,
Blythe Blue, Emerys Apple Green,
Colmans Jaffa Orange, Purple Brown
and 860 Yellow.

E 505

Cup 4 leaves from top edge.
interspersed with spray as on edge
of saucer. Inside cup and centre
of saucer solid Blue Green.
Handle half solid Purple Brown

Leaf Pattern in.
Blythe Blue, Jaffa Orange, 860 Yellow
Purple Brown, light Mixed Green, Hair Brown and
Black.
Plate. Four leaves, spray in centre.
Saucer. Four leaves, solid light Green in centre
Cup solid light Green inside 4 leaves outside
Handle. Jaffa Orange, Half solid.

E506

: C 22

C.C.25

: C 27

C C.26

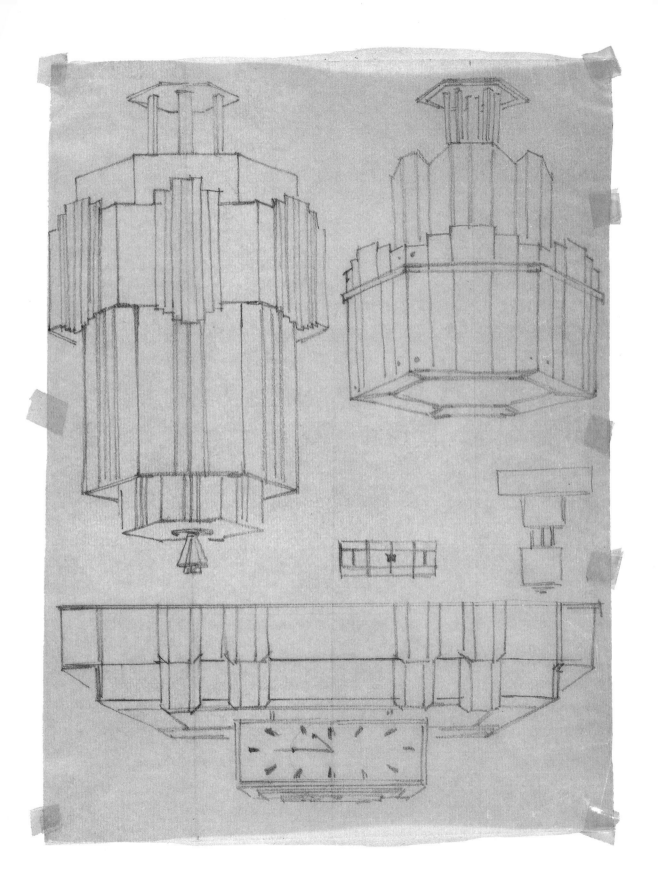

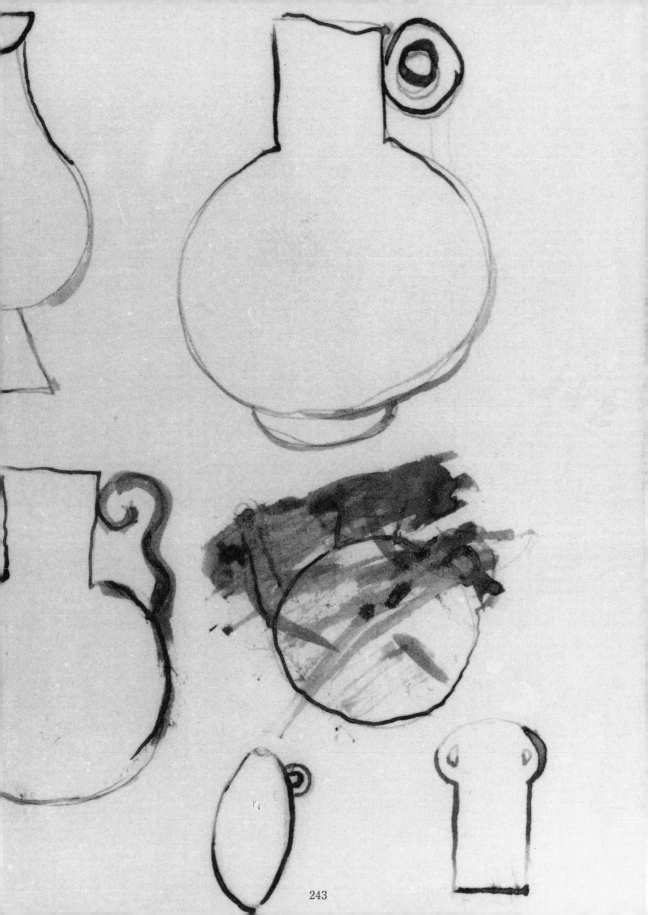

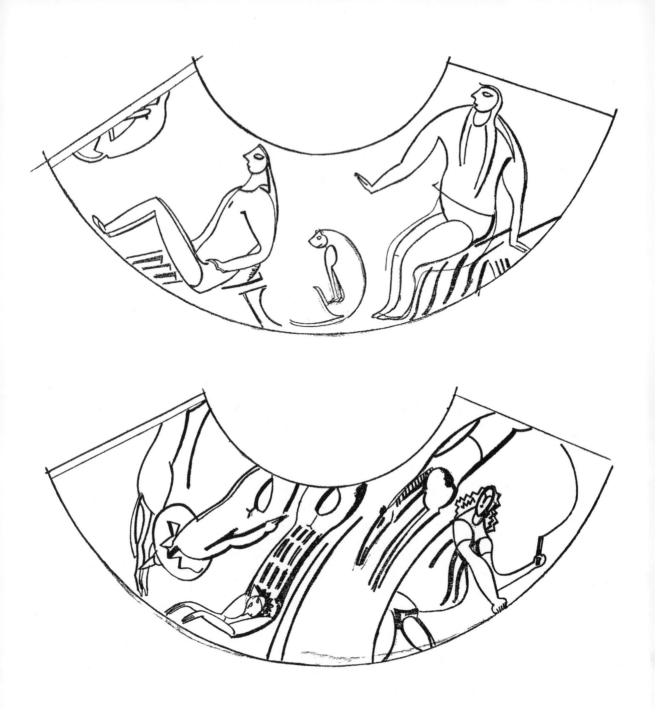

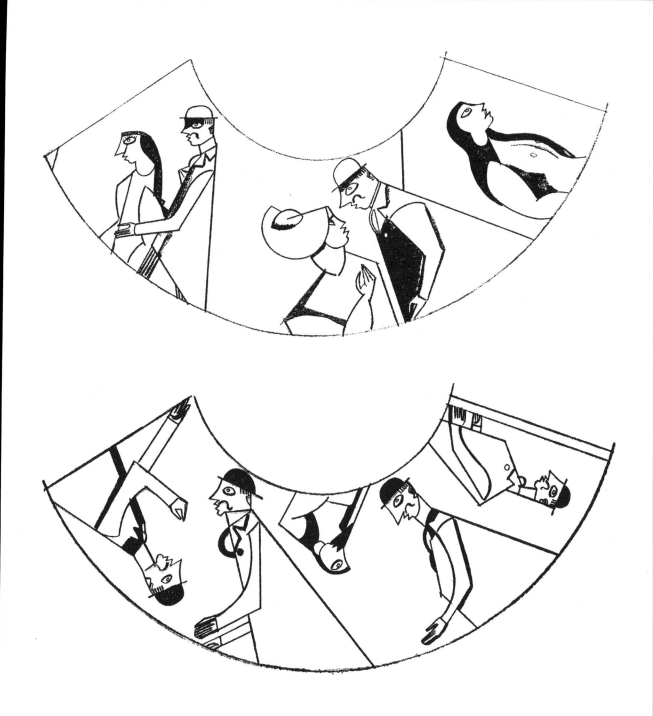

Select BIBLIOGRAPHY

Many of the volumes, records and documents from which the material reproduced in this book has been drawn are, by their very nature, unpublished and, in many cases, not immediately accessible. Indeed, the best possible bibliography for this book would be a complete listing of the archives and records held in public collections and by individual companies throughout England. The titles listed below are of those books which I would recommend for further reading.

Anscombe, Isabelle, *Omega and After: Bloomsbury and the Decorative Arts*, London, 1985

Atterbury, Paul (ed.), *A.W.N. Pugin: Master of Gothic Revival*, New York, 1995

Barrett, Helena and Phillips, John, *Suburban Style: The British Home 1840-1960*, London, 1987

Batkin, Maureen, *Wedgwood Ceramics 1846–1959*, London, 1982

Boynton, Lindsay (ed.), *Gillow Furniture Designs 1760–1800*, London, 1995

Calloway, Stephen, *The House of Liberty*, London, 1992

Catleugh, Jon, *William De Morgan Tiles*, Shepton Beauchamp, 1983

Cooper, Jeremy, *Victorian and Edwardian Interiors and Furniture*, London, 1987

Copeland, Robert, *Spode and Copeland Marks and Other Relevant Intelligence*, London, 1993

Durant, Stuart, *Christopher Dresser*, London, 1993

Evans, Wendy, Ross, Cathy and Werner, Alex, *Whitefriars Glass*, London, 1995

Forty, Adrian, *Objects of Desire: Design and Society 1750–1980*, London, 1986

Goodden, Susanna, *At the Sign of the Fourposter: The History of Heal's*, London, 1984

Griffin, Leonard and Meisel, Louis K., *Clarice Cliff: The Bizarre Affair*, London, 1988

Hoskins, Lesley (ed.), *The Papered Wall: The History and Techniques of Wallpaper*, London, 1994

MacCarthy, Fiona, *British Design Since 1880*, London, 1982

Meller, Susan and Elffers, Joost, *Textile Designs*, London, 1991

Parissien, Steven, *Adam Style*, London, 1992

Parissien, Steven, *Regency Style*, London, 1992

Parry, Linda, *Textiles of the Arts and Crafts Movement*, London, 1988

Parry, Linda, *William Morris Textiles*, London, 1983

Praz, Mario, *An Illustrated History of Interior Decoration From Pompeii to Art Nouveau*, London, 1964

Reilly, Robin, *Wedgwood: The New Illustrated Dictionary*, Woodbridge, 1995

Rothstein, Natalie, *Silk Designs of the Eighteenth Century*, London, 1990

The Silver Studio Collection: The London Design Studio 1880–1963, London, 1980

Slesin, Suzanne, Rozensztroch, Daniel and Cliff, Stafford, *Collecting Everyday Things: Kitchen Ceramics*, New York, 1997

Thornton, Peter, *Authentic Decor: The Domestic Interior 1620–1920*, London, 1984

Tilbrook, A.J., *The Designs of Archibald Knox for Liberty & Co.*, London, 1995

Youds, Bryn, *Susie Cooper: An Elegant Affair*, London, 1996

Picture CREDITS

INDEX

Author's ACKNOWLEDGMENTS

My very grateful thanks is due to all those who have helped in the preparation of this book, especially the staff at the many museums and archives who took the time and trouble to reply to our letters; in particular, I would like to thank the staff of the various departments of the Victoria & Albert Museum, especially Isobel Sinden and Martin Durrant in the Picture Library.

Of the many companies who opened their archives to me, my particular thanks goes to Lynn Miller at the Wedgwood Museum, Paul Wood and Stella McIntyre at the Spode Museum Trust, Terry Woolliscroft at Caradon Bathrooms Ltd., Graham Darby and Richard G. Pugh-Cook at Tomkinson's Carpets Ltd., Peter Ravenhill and Yvonne Smith at Woodward Grosvenor & Co. Ltd., and Andrew Priest who photographed the Woodward Grosvenor archive material for us.

I am indebted to Philip de Bay for his enthusiastic support of this project, for the use of his photographic archive and for taking many more photographs for us, and to Kulbir Thandi, who took the photographs of the Spode Archive reproduced on the preliminary pages of this book, to Sara Waterson who did a remarkable job of picture and source research, and to John Scott for his continued assistance, support, patience and knowledge.

Finally, my thanks go to the designers of the past whose work accidentally or deliberately ended up in the nation's archives; this is a testament to their labours, but is only a sample of the riches which they created. The *Artists' Papers Register* at the Henry Moore Institute in Leeds is attempting the near-impossible in making a detailed listing of the holdings of over 1000 repositories in England and Scotland, including libraries, museums, galleries, universities, societies and institutions.

If, as a designer, your appetite is whetted by the contents of this book, go and search out the original archives for yourself. I have only been able to show a fraction of what is stored away, but if the illustrations in this book prove a source of inspiration to you, as I hope they will, then consider carefully before you consign your own designs to the attic or the incinerator rather than to a repository, where they may form part of a remarkable heritage in the future.

First published in the United Kingdom in 1998 as *The English Archive of Design and Decoration* by Thames & Hudson Ltd, 181A High Holborn, London WC1V 7QX

www.thamesandhudson.com

© 1998 and 2008 Thames & Hudson Ltd, London
English Style and Decoration: A Sourcebook of Original Designs

British Library Cataloguing-in-Publication Data
A catalogue record for this book is available from the British Library
ISBN 978-0-500-51399-6

Printed and bound in China by C & C Offset Printing Co. Ltd.

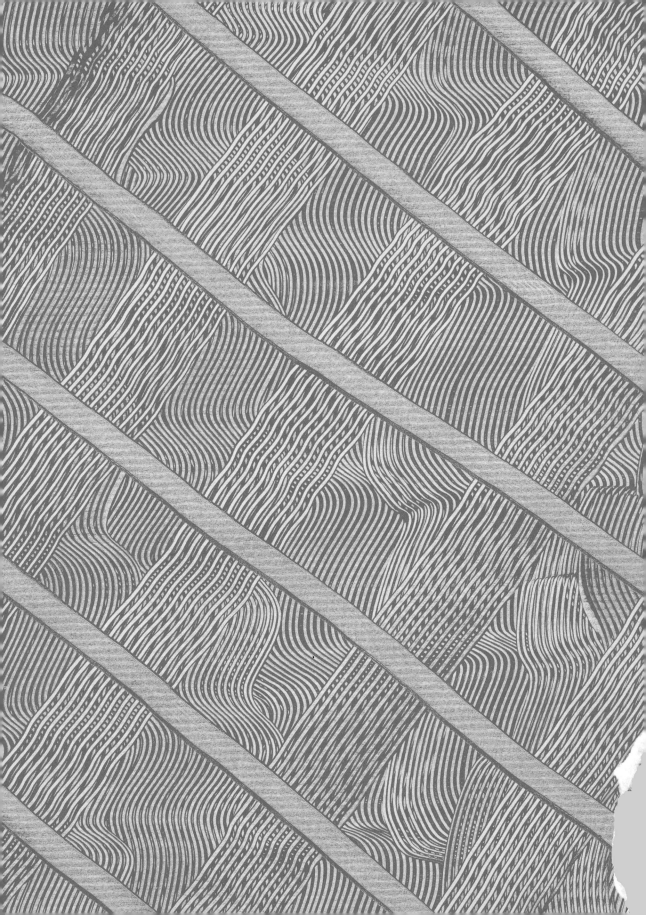